AF557819

THE WHOLE BEING

THE WHOLE BEING

A Journey Towards Harmony and Happiness

Rishi Kumar Mishra

RUPA
PUBLICATIONS INDIA
in association with
BRAHMA VIDYA KENDRA
NEW DELHI, INDIA

Published in 2011 by
Rupa Publications India Pvt. Ltd.
7/16, Ansari Road, Daryaganj,
New Delhi 110 002

Sales Centres:

Allahabad Bengaluru Chandigarh Chennai
Hyderabad Jaipur Kathmandu
Kolkata Mumbai

Printed in India by
Nutech Photolithographers
B-240, Okhla Industrial Area, Phase-I,
New Delhi 110 020, India

CONTENTS

SECTION ONE

~

PROLOGUE

PROLOGUE

The Whole Being: A Journey Towards Harmony and Happiness is the fifth in a series authored by RK Mishra that brings to light the practical wisdom enshrined in India's most ancient texts, the Vedas. The author also drew on the wisdom of 'modern science' for this work, notably the scientific understandings of a few visionaries which are of particular relevance to this book.

This fifth and final volume was intended to be the synthesis of the works preceding it. Its eminently practical purpose was to draw on the various facets explored in the previous volumes in order to demonstrate how Vedic understandings can assist today's troubled world. The author intended to reveal the 'blueprint' for a harmonious, balanced society that had been developed by the Vedic seer-scientists (*rishi*s) in the light of their intellectual and experiential knowledge of the true nature of the cosmos. The aim was to help the global community address some of the most pernicious social ills in the contemporary world and move towards a greater harmony and mutual understanding. Unfortunately, however, the current volume is incomplete as RK Mishra fell ill and passed away while it was still very much a work-in-progress.

His stated intention, as drawn up in a research framework, was indeed expansive. Lack of space prevents a full listing here of all the elements the author wished to explore, but even a brief summary serves to indicate both the sweeping breadth and the probing specificity of his research. For example, Mishraji intended to explore the historical evolution of and thought systems about mind and body. This exploration was to include physical, emotional, intellectual and spiritual health; the effect of the food cycle, seasons and psychology; and all relationships from the cosmic (sun, moon and stars and so forth) to the deeply personal, between man and woman, between elders and young people, between the individual and family. He would have included sections on the life cycle of birth to death to birth, and on allegory, metaphor and imagery. He wished to explore the impact upon an individual of the seasons, time, work, relationships, emotions, physical reactions to stimuli, and more. He was keen to look more deeply into Newtonian thought and methods of analysis, the Cartesian world view and medical science, relativity and quantum theory. And he wished to delve into our relationship with the natural world – the sun and the rains, the water cycle, and what we can (and should) learn from nature herself.

The Whole Being is preceded by: *Before the Beginning and After the End: Beyond the Universe of Physics – Rediscovering Ancient Insights* (2000), which addressed various aspects of creation and of the cosmos, including how the cosmos originated and what its future will be, the nature of the individual self and its place in the universe. This was followed by *The Cosmic Matrix: in the Light of the Vedas* (2001), which developed the study of the cosmos, exploring its subtlety, complexity, continuity and fluidity. The next volume in the series, *The Realm of Supraphysics: Mind, Energy and Matter in the Light of the Vedas* (2003), examines the 'supraphysical' dimension (the domain of the subtle, all-pervasive forces underlying material reality) of the intimate relationship between mind, energy and matter. The fourth volume is *The Ultimate Dialogue: the Fusion of Knowledge, Intelligence and Action* (2007), a study of the deeper meaning and message of Bhagavadgita.

The Ultimate Dialogue steers seekers towards the process of overcoming fragmentation within our inner universe and its interface with the outer universe. This paves the way to achieving wholeness of being, in itself an essential prerequisite for establishing harmony and happiness, the pointers to ultimate bliss. The summary on the back cover of that volume includes the sentence: 'Our purpose here is to examine the factors which cause our unhappiness and to explore the path leading to inner harmony and balance.' Mishraji's intention in *The Whole Being*, as its title implies, was to extend and expand the exploration undertaken in *The Ultimate Dialogue* towards actualising inner harmony, happiness and balance in our 'outer life' in our society, our nation and the global community.

To this end, early in this millennium Mishraji and I commenced research on a number of key areas pertaining to the way we live our lives today. We began to trace the historical development of systems of thought on education, health care, man's relationship to woman, and humankind's relationship to the natural environment. This was to form the basis for understanding how the current fragmentary, segmented view of existence came about, and would then have been compared with the holistic understanding of the *rishis*. The author also wished to explore how our world would be if this fragmentation had not occurred, and to articulate the significance of each of the six limbs of the Vedas and of this corpus in its totality.

This endeavour was interrupted by Mishraji's ill-health; regrettably we were unable to conclude the research and he was unable to accomplish the comparison in written form. However, readers may catch a glimpse of this intention – and how it would have been borne out throughout this work – in Section 7, wherein two important facets of life are examined in the light of Vedic understanding. These are: the foundation and processes of communication; and the much misunderstood and maligned principle of *varna*.

As Mishraji's book editor for the whole series, it has been a privilege (as well as an immensely sad task) to prepare this unfinished manuscript for publication. I have felt his absence keenly and often. In previous years I would always receive a considered response from him when I requested clarification of profound Vedic principles in the chapters he sent to me for editing. Yet in the endeavour of preparing this volume for publication, I have been invaluably assisted by Renuka Mishra, wife of late RK Mishra and by his personal assistant for many years, CM Jayanji, who proof-read the previous three volumes. We are conscious of the inadequacies of this manuscript – not only because it is incomplete, but also because much of it was still in draft stage or written afresh as late as 2008 when Mishraji was terminally ill. Yet simultaneously we are aware that this book has many jewels to offer its readers, and thus we decided to publish it.

At an earlier stage, when he was well, RK Mishra had written a pertinent introduction, presented here as Section 2, which lays the foundations for the rest of the book. He proceeds to elucidate the truth of wholeness as evidenced in the Vedas so beautifully, in Sections 3 and 4, that this text has required only the lightest editorial touch. In section 5, he explores the concept of wholeness in the eastern tradition by way of the examples of Kashmiri Shaivism and the Soka Gokkai Japanese school of Buddhism. And in Section 6, he introduces readers to the revelatory insights of three independent thinkers in the so-called 'modern world': Goethe, Viktor Schauberger and David Bohm. Although he had intended to present their work in more detail, this section is valuable even in its incomplete form. For it gives us hope. While society generally subscribes to the fragmentary, compartmentalised view of reality that has created such serious problems for our lives and our planet, there will always be courageous and visionary individuals such as these three, whose scientific discoveries come close to the understanding of reality divined and tested by the Vedic seer-scientists.

The Truth itself doesn't change. RK Mishra, his guru Pandit Motilal Shastri, and Motilal Shastri's guru Pandit Madhusudan Ohja knew that the Truth enshrined in the Vedas has timeless relevance. Now, perhaps more than ever before, we need the wisdom of the Vedas to illuminate the path ahead.

Melbourne, Australia — Vyvyan Mishra (née Cayley)
28 September 2010

SECTION TWO

~

THE WHOLE BEING

Chapter 1

THE WHOLE BEING

पूर्णमदः पूर्णमिदं पूर्णात्पूर्णमुदच्यते।
पूर्णस्य पूर्णमादाय पूर्णमेवावशिष्यते।।

That is whole,
This is whole,
That is infinite,
This is infinite,
When infinite is taken out of infinity
What remains is infinite.

– 'Peace Invocation', *Īśāvāsya Upaniṣad*

'That' is a pronoun denoting something remote; it means the universal consciousness, also described as the Absolute or the Supreme *Brahman*. *That* Brahman, the ultimate source from which this entire creation of sentient and insentient beings originate, exist and finally merge into, is infinite, and *this* (universe) is infinite. The infinite proceeds from the infinite. (Then) it embraces the infinitude of the infinite (universe), and remains as the infinite alone.

That macrocosm is infinite, so is this microcosm. *That* universal consciousness is infinite, so is *this* individualised consciousness.

That is infinite, not limited by anything. In other words, that is all-pervading. *This* is something close, this universe. It is complete, all-pervading like space and unconditioned. That manifests itself through name and form. That is the cause. This microcosm, the individual, the effect, proceeds or emanates from the infinite. It does not give up its nature, infinitude. Taking the infinitude of the infinite, it attains perfect unity with its own nature by removing, through knowledge, its apparent otherness. The illusion of otherness is created by ignorance through the contact of limiting adjuncts, the elements.

The manifested effect is also infinite or real in the present moment. In all three stages of origin, continuance and dissolution, the cause and effect are infinite. There is just one infinity, spoken of as divided into cause and effect. For instance, an ocean consists of water, waves, foam, bubbles and so forth. Just as the water is real, so are its effects – the waves, foam and so on – which appear and disappear but are part and parcel of the ocean itself and are real. Similarly, the Supreme Brahman can be compared to the water of the ocean; and the entire, apparently dual universe is absolutely real.

This universe is not merely a sum of its parts. It is a whole. And it comprises innumerable entities which are whole in themselves. Probing a little deeper, we discover that such statements are somewhat inexact. To say that this universe as a whole is comprised of numerous entities that are whole in themselves is rather like saying that the ocean is made of waves and waves are made of water. For they are not separate entities; they are one and the same, albeit in different 'states of being'.

All metaphors partly reflect the reality they seek to communicate and partly deviate from it. The ocean-wave-water example does help us to understand what we are seeking to communicate; yet at the same time it does not exactly reflect reality. If we take water out of waves or waves out of the ocean, nothing will remain; whereas in the case of the universe, the wholeness is inexhaustible and infinite. It is said that if we take 'infinite' out of 'infinity' it will remain infinite. Take zero out of zero; what remains is zero. Add zero to zero; we get zero. The result is zero when we multiply zero with zero or divide zero by zero.

Let us return to the example of the universe which, as we said above, is complete in itself. We can visualise it as a perfect circle consisting of innumerable concentric circles, each of which is a whole, complete in itself. These concentric circles are infinite. Imagine them floating in infinite space: take out one circle – what remains is the whole. All circles, including concentric circles, have a centre. Even the tiniest of circles has an infinitesimally tiny circle, a point. Each circle is connected with the other circles, as if 'in the womb' of progressively larger circles.

On occasions it is necessary to investigate and discuss each circle separately. Problems arise, however, when we come to believe that they really are separate from each other. Similarly, we can take some water from the sea and put it in a container. The separateness arises because of the container. If we later remove the cause of separateness – the container – we find that all water is the same. This cause is the conditioning which creates the illusion of diversity in unity.

Such diversity is often perceived as posing a problem to those who seek wholeness, for its various outlooks, differences in theoretical formulation and conflicts of philosophical expression appear to be contradictory. In fact, there is no contradiction; these perceived differences in presentation and articulation are simply diverse paths leading to the same destination.

From time immemorial, sages, seers and scientists have articulated this principle in their inimitable and diverse ways. The Vedic seers and scholars explain wholeness at various levels, ranging from that of an individual to the cosmos, from microcosm to macrocosm. According to these sages, the universe comprises innumerable individuals, each of which is an entity possessing a name, form and function. Each individual is a whole, a unique circle which is part of the innumerable concentric circles floating in space; and all individuals are interconnected. The term 'connection' may create the impression that two separate individuals are somehow physically 'linked' to each other; but this is not so. Rather, each individual is an aspect of infinity, the whole within which all these concentric circles are located.

The Descent into Fragmentation

Before the advent of organised religions, human beings and nature were engaged in a mutually nourishing embrace of wholeness. Later, however, as religious movements began to segregate believers from non-believers, people gradually moved away from nature, discarding the natural laws and becoming disconnected from the harmony inherent in the 'natural' way of life. Over time, the drift away from the basic principles of wholeness became acute, and the human intellect came under the spell of a fragmentary approach. Social norms began to violate the principles and practice of a spontaneous and natural partnership between men and women. The invigorating bonds between human beings and nature, between the individual and society, and between microcosm and macrocosm were ruptured. This process was aggravated as the 'religion' of reason and rationality began to gain influence; and this trend gathered further momentum with the advent of what is hailed as the age of 'modern' science.

Under the influence of the Newtonian world view, people came to visualise the universe as a machine, to understand which it was necessary to break it down into parts and then examine each part. As this endeavour continued, increasingly sophisticated tools were developed to enable examination of ever smaller and more intricate parts of the whole. But it was discovered that, while human understanding of even the tiniest parts improved, the capacity to understand the whole had deserted us. Then a stage was reached when 'modern science' told us that human beings are incapable of knowing reality because the act of observing reality brings about a change in reality. Gradually, some modern 'scientists' began to look to the eastern world view in an attempt to understand reality; but the prolonged internalisation of looking at the universe as a sum of its parts had brought about a fragmentation of the human capacity to comprehend the whole.

In fact, some modern physicists are becoming increasingly restless in the face of a continuing denial of wholeness in favour of the promotion of fragmentation. Some of these scientists are even rising in revolt against the widely-acclaimed infallibility of verifiable 'truth'. There is a growing realisation that the assertion that 'truth' must validate itself on the touchstone of verification is often a product of power-play at a particular period of human history. This explains why 'truth' often changes with alterations in the power equation. The lives and experience of Copernicus, Galileo and the like are eloquent examples of highly-acclaimed assertions about the infallibility of verifiable 'truths'.

On occasion, these assertions are revealed to be nothing more than an exercise in self-deception, as a 'new' truth overturns an 'old' truth; the latest example of this is the fate of the Newtonian world view. The ostensible process of verification on the touchstone of 'scientific methods' is fundamentally flawed, because it operates on a basis of blunting or paralysing the subtle, sophisticated tools of verification which have been available to human beings for several millennia. These comprehensive tools rely upon human faculties beyond those of the senses and their technological extensions; but over the centuries they have been suppressed and overtaken by various devices, such as the use of economic, political and military power, and by the development of sophisticated tools of 'mind-management'.

An element to be noted is the much-celebrated worship of the new creed of 'scientific temper', which describes an attitude that involves the application of logic and the avoidance of biased and preconceived notions. Discussion, argument and analysis are vital parts of scientific temper. It is thus necessarily open, admitting every point of view, however heterodox and regardless of its point of origin.

The concept of scientific temper flows from the view that modern science has given people vast knowledge, and this knowledge has brought immense power. But this knowledge is used by people, who wield the power derived from that knowledge and who make choices upon which the course of science and the future destiny of humanity depend. If, as is assumed today, the crisis that humanity faces is a moral one, this can only be an outcome of the conflict within human beings themselves. For, while science dominates the western world and is widely paid tribute by its citizens, it must be acknowledged that the West is still far from having developed the real temper of science. It has still to bring the spirit and the flesh into creative harmony.

The Journey Back to Wholeness

Various concepts of wholeness are vividly discernible in the world views articulated by the *rishis*, and are also reflected in the arts of Bharatavarsha. Thus culture, thought, science, ritual and spirituality are like branches of a vast tree, which cannot be understood in isolation. They are based on the fundamental concepts of the cosmos and of humanity, of space and time, of the body, mind and self. Theories of aesthetics rest on philosophical concepts but are deeply linked with medical experience and that which is often described by the modern mind as 'mystical experience'.

As part of our study of concepts of wholeness, we shall be considering the following aspects: the various dimensions encompassing the past, present and future, and the different stages of life – birth, growth, ageing, and death; how undifferentiated sound is woven in a matrix of wholeness as it travels to become articulated speech; how the three apparently different states of waking, dream and deep sleep are, in fact, three dimensions of a unified universal consciousness; and how human beings and nature embrace each other in a spirit of wholeness. We shall also examine the irreparable damage that has been caused by modern fragmentary thought processes, which serve to seriously undermine these numerous strands of unity and harmony. We examine these and other, associated concepts and aspects with the intention of drawing the portrait of a whole being, as distinct from a fragmented being, and to explore the ways in which we can arrest the process of fragmentation, both at the conceptual as well as the practical level.

Fragmentation is the cause of all confusion and conflict and, ultimately, of human unhappiness. Despite our familiarity with a state of fragmentation in the modern world, there is a deeper impulse in us which seeks wholeness, and hence much thought, discussion and debate occurs around this subject.

True moral values – which alone can survive the outward changes brought about by the impact of science and the explosion of scientific knowledge – belong to wisdom. The need of the hour is for people of wisdom. Mere knowledge without wisdom to guide us in the utilisation of that knowledge will only bring greater sorrow.

The intention behind this work is to arrest and reverse the process of observed fragmentation in our universe. In doing so, we attempt to rejuvenate the human capacity to comprehend the whole, and to use that comprehension as a practical tool. By reversing this perspective of fragmentation and developing our latent potential to comprehend that we are a whole being, we begin the journey towards enduring happiness and harmony in the universe.

SECTION THREE

~

ENGAGING WITH WHOLENESS

Chapter 2

BEGINNING WITH 'I'

We can begin the process of engaging with wholeness from wherever we feel comfortable. Since everything – every phenomenon and every individual – is connected, the process of embracing wholeness can begin at any point in time and space, at any juncture in human life, and with any aspect of knowledge. Infinity has no beginning and no end; it is vast, endless space, a shoreless ocean. Therefore, we can begin with a drop, with a wave, with a tide, or with the vast sheet of water spreading out towards the horizon. In this process we will also notice that the horizon is not a location, but is merely the limit of our vision. The more we move towards the horizon, the more it recedes. The greater the distance that we are able to see, the more the horizon expands.

For the sake of convenience we shall begin our endeavour with an entity close to us, which is ourselves. So, who is this 'I'?[1] How is it a whole, and how is it part of a whole? When we look at 'I', the first aspect we see is the body, constituted of skin, flesh, blood, marrow, limbs and so on. When we say 'this is "my" book', we are stating that 'I' and the 'book' are two entities. So when I say '"my" body', I am also making the statement that 'I' and 'my body' are two separate entities, albeit bound together in a certain relationship. But is this true?

Continuing our search for the 'I' we notice that, unlike stones or other insentient objects, 'my body' has some extra qualities. It can perform several functions such as eating, grasping, reproducing, breathing and so forth. We attribute this to the fact that 'my body' has life. Breath, or the vital air, is the source of this life, and when this air is sucked out – when inhaling and exhaling cease – 'my body' becomes like a lifeless stone. We begin to wonder, therefore, if the combination of body and vital air is actually 'me'.

The pleasure of having thus discovered 'my' self is short-lived, for we note that other bodies – such as worms, insects and animals – also perform the same functions that we do. We also discover the fact that, unlike stones, 'my body' grows and changes. Yet change is not 'my' unique quality either, for a simple seed sprouts into a plant and grows into a tree. So we continue our search, until we arrive at something that definitely appears to be the defining attributes of 'my body'. 'My body' has sense capacities; it can hear, touch, see, taste and smell. These sense capacities tell us that we have found what 'I' is. We relax. Now we know that 'I' is the combination of body, life-force, sense capacities and mind.

But then we realise that although sense capacities are integral to the body, we do not always perceive things with our senses even when they are clearly within range. As I am returning from a walk in the garden, my wife asks me: 'Did you see the beautiful bougainvillea?' and I have to admit that I did not, because my mind was preoccupied with a problem in my office. I literally did not see what was before my eyes. It is only when the mind floats through the sense capacities and reaches objects that we perceive them. Nevertheless, perhaps we can simply expand our definition, and state that 'I' is the combination of the sense capacities and the mind, along with the vital air or life-force and the physical body. So what happens, then, when I am in deep sleep? It appears that the sense capacities cease to function in that state. Do 'I' still exist? It would appear so.

Reflection continues. Is this definition of 'I' adequate? We begin to discern that animals also have a body, action capacities and sense capacities. They have feelings, which fluctuate as ours do. After a while, we recognise the distinction that human beings are endowed with an intellect, the faculty of discriminating between right and wrong. When my mind exhibits an impulse to rush in a wayward direction, my intellect halts it, advises it and steers it towards the right path. This intellect, it would appear, is the defining distinction between 'I' and other entities, both sentient and insentient. Even though some animals do possess intelligence, there is no comparison with the quality and scale of human intelligence.

Having reached this juncture a door suddenly opens, as it were. We 'realise' that 'I', or 'self', is something different from body, life-force, mind or intellect. And this fact is infinite, because it relates to every entity in the universe – 'my' book, 'my' wife, 'my' friend. This realisation of the self frees us from the ignorance which had made us, in the first instance, identify 'I' with 'my body'. This, therefore, is the centre of the concentric circle which holds together the other concentric circles of body, life-force, mind and intellect.

But, as we shall discover, this is the centre of a set of concentric circles which are integral to another set of concentric circles. This is consciousness at the level of an individual. But there is another, universal dimension of consciousness.

This self is infinite, and it is the same in every individual; it is the point at the centre of concentric circles. In itself it is unlimited, but it is conditioned by the limitations of the intellect. For although the human intellect may be thought of as vast – at least in its potential – it is relatively limited in comparison with the unlimited expanse of the self.

This self is, in a sense, witness to what 'I' am doing. It is not the doer, although we commonly assume that it is the doer because of its association with the intellect, mind and body. The hub of the wheel does not move even while the axle, wheels and whole car move. 'I' am not moving; 'I' am a witness to the movement. When we recognise this self as witness, we are able to remove the ignorance that the 'I' is the body, mind or intellect.

Waking, Dreaming and Deep Sleep

We experience the self vividly when we witness ourselves in the three states of waking, dream, and deep sleep. An enquiry into these three states of experience reveals the real nature of 'I', the individualised consciousness or self. Most philosophical systems analyse life in its waking state, but a truly holistic perspective involves the study of life and consciousness in all three states.

An analysis of the waking state shows that the 'I' or individual self resides in a physical body and employs its instruments to enjoy the objects of the external world. But the 'I' is not the body; the self is not non-self. The former is conscious while the latter is inert. In the dreaming state, the 'I' (self) creates a world of its own from the impressions of its waking experience. It doesn't need the help of the sense organs nor of external light. In the dreaming state, the self reveals itself in a world of images, and its experiences are subtle. It is unattached in dreams; even though it appears to roam far and wide and play with many objects, it does not really act. When we awake, we realise that we haven't actually done anything or gone anywhere. Thus the dreaming state reveals that the 'I' can create an entire universe without the need of an external 'light' to do so.

When we dream, we have no use for our external sense organs. Just as a sword shines when withdrawn from its sheath, similarly the knower, separated in the dreaming state from cause and effect, is seen to be self-effulgent. In dreams, the intellect by itself takes on the role of the doer, owing to the various residual impressions arising from the waking state. There are no cars there, no roads, no physical objects. The dreamer carries the impressions of these things from the world of waking and fashions cars, roads and so on, in the process creating a world in the dream. The consciousness moves, as it were, out of its nest (the physical body) and returns to itself, while the breath preserves the body. The objects and enjoyments in dreams are all constructed by the 'I'. There the self is its own illuminator.

Just as a hawk, having flown around here and there in space, becomes weary, folds its wings and is drawn to its nest, so the self hastens to that state where, asleep, it desires no desires and sees no visions. All distinctions fade out. This is the state of deep sleep, wherein there are no experiences, no desires, no objects, no dreams. The self is one, without the distinction of seer and seen. There is no knower, no knowing, no process of knowledge. The very ideas of 'within' and 'without' carry no meaning here. There is no seeing of objects, and yet sight remains.

An analysis of the deep sleep state shows that the self is relationless. In this state, all empirical distinctions vanish. There is no knowing subject nor known objects. Objective consciousness has disappeared, even while pure consciousness remains.

In the next chapter we delve more deeply into the nature of the 'I' or self and its relationship with the physical body and with the universe.[2]

Chapter 3

FROM BODY TO CONSCIOUSNESS

As we look more deeply into the nature of the 'I' or 'self', we begin to see how all the dimensions of 'I' may be visualised as external coatings or sheaths, in which the essence of reality is wrapped. The subtlest of the subtle – the principle of truth – resides within us as a spark, enveloped, as it were, by several grosser coatings of matter, the grossest being our physical body.

Just as the sheath of a sword merely encases the blade, so too is the reality within untouched by the sheaths covering it. The five sheaths described by the Vedic seer-scientists are: the gross physical structure of the anatomical form; the vital-air sheath of the physiological form; the mental sheath of the psychological form; the intellectual sheath; and the innermost sheath of bliss. As the sheaths move 'inwards' from gross to subtle, our true nature comes to be cognised as all-pervasive intelligence.

We begin with the body, which is the gross physical structure of the anatomical form. Thus, this body, with which we mistakenly tend to identify, is known as 'the gross body' for it contains the five 'gross material elements' of space, air, fire, water and earth, in varying proportions. (The word 'elements' is used here not in the sense that it is employed in modern physics but according to the meaning given to it in the Vedic lexicon. 'Material element' is a technical term for the primary building blocks of the universe on the material plane – the other planes being the physical and supraphysical.) Having united with parts of one another, these gross material elements combine to form the gross body. These elements are related to the five sense capacities of sound, touch, form or colour, taste and smell, which are, in turn, related to the sense objects. Sense objects are pleasing, displeasing or neutral. The moment we come in contact with a sense object, we begin to experience attachment and desire, aversion, or indifference.

When we mistakenly identify with our limited, finite body, we are led into often frantic attempts to secure unlimited, infinite happiness from this body alone. In pursuit of this, further sense gratifications are sought, involving the acquisition of pleasant objects and the dismissal of unpleasant objects. But, as we know, such a search for happiness through identification of the 'I' with the body only leads to frustration, because the physical body is inevitably and necessarily doomed to disappearance. Birth, growth, decay and death are the body's fate. In contrast, real happiness comes through freedom from birth, growth, decay and death. This is the meaning of liberation from bondage, which arises when the knowledge that one has been living in ignorance gives way to the thought, 'I want to stop living in ignorance; I want to be free.'

Our conception of the outer world is gained through our organs. The ears, skin, eyes, nose and tongue are known as the organs of knowledge, for they bring knowledge of external objects. The mouth, hands, feet, anus and genitals are the organs of action because of their tendency to work in particular ways within the body. In addition to these organs of knowledge and action, the body is also endowed with vital energy (*prana*), which descends into it from the supraphysical energy permeating the cosmos.[3]

The enjoyments of pleasure and pain related to our physical body are determined by our past actions. Thought by thought, action by action, we have caused the present body and mental capacities; and even while we are alive and acting here and now, we are ordering the 'shape' of our future existence. It is up to us to decide our future; we can attain a better life with plenty of opportunities for steady progress, or we can descend into a greater gloom. With our own actions we form a blueprint for the exact shape of our destiny. This is because our actions are caused by desires, both spontaneous and stimulated, which leave imprints on our mind. These imprints propel us to act accordingly. The more we act under the influence of these impulses the stronger they become, and over the course of time they become entrenched. This is often referred to as 'second nature'.

Our mental sheath is kept blazing by the fuel of these impulses. Thoughts are only imaginations of the mind, expressed in the form of agitations. When the sense organs bring the stimuli to our mind, it becomes more 'ablaze' or agitated, and these agitations manifest as activities in the world. The mind cannot be controlled unless the sense organs are controlled; and the sense organs cannot be controlled unless their fields are controlled. The mind causes our attachment to our body and the objects of our senses. These attachments bind us like an animal tied with a rope. Similarly, when the infinite consciousness is (apparently) bound by the three modes of nature namely *sattva*, *rajas* and *tamas*, it seems to have lost its omnipotence and omniscience and to have become limited, individualised consciousness.

The ordinary mind is fickle and ever-changing – at one moment sorrowful, at another excited and joyful. This mind is the cause for all sense objects; as the objects constantly change, so too must the mind constantly change, to 'become' the objects. Thus, the effects are nothing other than the cause in another form. Mind can only conceive things known. What I do not know, I cannot think about. The moment I gain a new piece of knowledge, it becomes a new idea to think about. The present boundaries of my knowledge are the outermost frontiers to which my mind can pervade.

However, seekers of ultimate reality discover that these apparent 'outermost frontiers' are, in fact, illusory. A mountain is limited by space; the sun is limited by direction. But our knowledge, or awareness, is unlimited. It is able to embrace a small seed as well as a huge mountain with equal ease. When we look at a seed our awareness assumes the form of a seed, and when we look at a mountain our awareness expands to embrace the mountain. When we look at a vast ocean, we find our awareness extending accordingly. In fact, our knowledge or awareness is able to encompass and embrace the entire universe, including past, present and future. Objects floating in awareness may vanish, but awareness or knowledge remains, for it is that luminous aspect of our selves which is unconditioned by time, space or location. Knowledge, or awareness, is the seer, the witness in us.

To put it another way, knowledge is unconditioned while the known is conditioned. The *rishi*s have expressed these two aspects using the terms *Brahma* and karma. Knowledge is the eternal and unconditioned, Brahma; and karma is the ever-changing object of knowledge, that which is known (such as hills, rivers, the sun, the moon). Together, these two comprise the foundation of the universe and are intertwined. The eternal aspect is subsumed in the ever-changing aspect, and the transitory aspect resides in the enduring aspect.

Knowledge, Knower and Known

When I say to my friend, 'Look at this book,' my observation clearly comprises two components: (a) that the book exists; and (b) that I know the book exists. Examining more deeply, the statement actually confirms three, rather than two aspects: the existence (of the book), the knowledge (of the existence of the book), and the object that exists (the book).

The universe is a whole comprised of these three aspects, which in themselves complete a circle: existence, consciousness of existence, and the knowledge thereof. When we have the desire to know something and are able to fulfil that desire, great joy is the fruit. This joy comes from the satisfaction of the desire to know and brings with it an end to our restlessness, so that we experience peace. This satisfaction, or joy, is the sustaining elixir of life. The *rishis* call it bliss (*ananda*), which one experiences on knowing oneself, on attaining self-realisation. A significant depletion in this life-force is a sign that we are close to bidding goodbye to this world.

Even if the self escapes objectification, it does not escape certainty. Nothing is more certain than the fact of one's own existence. It is self-evident, immediate and direct. One may doubt many things, but one can never doubt one's own being – because the act of doubting would be an affirmation of one's very existence. The self cannot be proved since it is the basis of all proof and is established prior to all proofs. How can that by which all the means of valid knowledge are established itself be established by the means of valid knowledge? That by which this universe is pervaded, but which nothing pervades; which is not of the nature of effulgence yet shines – that is the self or consciousness. It is the one by whose very presence the body, sense organs, mind and intellect keep to their respective functions, like servants obeying their master. This, truly, is the 'I'.

Every individual comprising the universe is endowed with all three facets of existence, consciousness, and the object of existence and consciousness. Nothing is beyond these three; although we consider them as three aspects for the purposes of analysis or discussion, in reality they are intimately interwoven and constitute a composite whole. They are not three fragments put together by an artificial device. Where there is existence, there is consciousness of that existence; and if we are conscious of that existence, there must be an individual which exists and of which we are conscious.

A close examination of individuals (defined in the Vedas as objects and entities with form, name and function) reveals the presence of numerous individuals within any one individual. For instance, we normally consider a tree as a single individual or object. But when we examine it more closely, each tree has numerous leaves, each leaf has numerous veins, and each vein is an aggregate of numerous atoms, molecules and particles. Each is distinct from the other, yet forms an inextricable part of the whole. Numerous branches spread out above the ground, reaching for the sky; underneath the ground, equally numerous branches (the roots of the tree) reach for the centre of the earth. The aggregate of these innumerable branches is what we call a 'tree'. Although these innumerable aspects are distinct from each other, they are also akin to the different movements of a single dance. Even the smallest particle in our world comprises these numerous aspects, as do the largest of objects or individuals.

Existence is the common factor. Once we are able to comprehend this fact, it becomes easier to understand the two other dimensions of knowledge and the object of knowledge. The word 'is' signifies existence, and is common to all statements, such as 'this is a pot', 'this is a book', 'this is a horse', and so on. This determinant of existence, the term 'is', is even present in the formulation that 'there is no book'. Thus, we see that existence is all-pervasive. Knowledge and the object of that knowledge are inexorably interwoven with this 'factor' of existence. We gain knowledge of something when we comprehend that it exists.

Objects in the world exist as a consequence of the balance between liking and disliking, being perceived as desirable or undesirable, beneficial or harmful, and so forth. As humans, we tend to like sweet things and dislike poison; we like a beautiful garden and dislike snakes. We perceive some objects as being useful and others as being useless or harmful. Yet there are some things that we reject in one context but which become useful, and therefore acceptable, in another. For example, we believe that human waste deserves to be discarded; yet it is useful as a fertiliser for crops. This process of 'transformation' from uselessness to usefulness, and vice versa, continues incessantly. These two are also different aspects of a single individual rather than being contradictory realities. All transactions in the world are caused by the interaction between these two opposing tendencies.

Every individual is endowed with its own inherent nature. Water has a cooling nature, while the nature of fire is to generate heat. If we place an individual in a situation contrary to its inherent nature, it will enter a state of disorder. For instance, if we were to take two containers filled with water and put one on a fire and the other in snow, we would quickly become unable to pick up either container without experiencing severe discomfort or pain. Both extremes of temperature disrupt the harmony of the water. When we remove the cause of the disruption, the water will return to its normal nature.

The state of equipoise is the ability to recognise these factors and act accordingly, so as to experience peace and tranquillity. This process of balancing the factors that disturb the normal nature of an individual brings peace, because it signifies respecting and adhering to the principle of wholeness.

Chapter 4

CONTINUITY AND CHANGE

When we observe an individual (object or entity), we find that it is changing every moment. The object we see today is not the same as the one we saw yesterday, nor will it be the same tomorrow. The continuous process of change taking place in every individual is usually not discernible to the observer as it is not noticeable superficially. But those with a 'scientific' eye – an insight to look beyond the obvious, piercing the superficial – are able to recognise this continuous change taking place in every individual that possesses a name, form and function.

For example, the body is an aggregate of blood, flesh, bones, marrow and so on, and each of these aspects is subject to change, decay and degeneration. A baby's body grows into a tall adult with muscular strength and energy before, with advancing age, it again loses strength and becomes feeble. These changes occur because of changes in the components that comprise the body, as mentioned before – flesh, bones, marrow and so forth.

We can also think of the example of the waves in an ocean. Water changes into foam, which changes into salt, which changes into sand, which changes into stone, which changes into iron; and from iron, gold is formed. Thus, by a process of churning and consolidation, water is transformed into all of these different objects. This transformation is taking place continuously. It would be silly to ask at what point of time water becomes a wave or wave becomes sand.

Or let us consider a strong wooden door that cannot be broken today even by a strong hammer. In 200 years time, if someone were to just take hold of a part of it, that part would come away in their hands. It is impossible to locate the particular moment when that hard wooden door will change into pieces. This process of change never stops.

We may bathe in the river Ganges at a particular spot, and it may occur to us to reflect that, say, ten years earlier someone else was bathing here, at the exact same spot in this mighty river. But the water that was flowing then is no longer here, and we cannot say where it has gone. The river, however, as the aggregate, is the same as it was a moment ago and as it was ten years ago. Someone did bathe in the Ganges 100 years ago, at this same spot, and someone else will bathe here 100 years from now. The water in which we three people have bathed is different, but the Ganges is the factor of continuity.

At a deeper level, the universe appears to be without beginning or an end; it is infinite. Yet it comprises innumerable individuals – objects and entities with name, form and function – and each of these is in the process of incessant change. Thus, we witness apparently contradictory aspects in our universe – an enduring aspect and one of continuous change. Existence is a whole, made up of these two aspects – continuity and change – which co-exist in harmony.

When we recognise this aspect of existence to be true, it does not constrict us but rather frees us. Liberating knowledge is gained not by going beyond appearances but by attending closely to them. True knowledge, from this point of view, is the realisation that apparent opposites normally contrasted with one another are aspects of the same reality. These include such apparent opposites as subject and object, unity and diversity, absolute and relative. All the categories of existence are present in every single category. One who realises this experiences every particular individual as the sum total of everything else, and recognises that all things have one nature. This is the essence or co-extensive unity of all things. Readers will meet this truth again and again in the pages of this book, for both ancient schools of thoughts and individual 'thinkers' in the modern world have come to recognise the reality we have met already in these first few pages.

Insofar as they share a common basis, a given cluster of appearances manifests as a single whole, in which any one may assume a more important or subordinate role. The result is a specific awareness of the form of an object. While individual appearances do not lose their separate identity when they rest on a common basis, the particular object which appears according to its own characteristics is an individual reality in its own right. They unite with each other in much the same way as the scattered rays of a lamp come together when focused, or as the various currents of the sea together give rise to waves. Atomic appearances can combine in any number of ways, provided that they are not contrary to one another as established by the dictates of natural law.

The form our experience assumes depends not only on the nature of the object perceived, but also on personal factors entirely peculiar to ourselves. Ignorance is the failure to experience directly the intimate connection between the infinite and the finite. The finite is a symbol of the infinite, and the infinite stamps its seal onto its own nature replete with all possible forms of the finite.

Chapter 5

REFLECTIONS

This section was originally published in RK Mishra's first book, Before the Beginning and After the End. *We reprint it here as a vibrant illustration of his profound understanding of the wholeness at the heart of the universe.*

What exactly is the beginning? And when does the end come?

More precisely, when do I come to discern a beginning? When do I notice that the end has come?

There is nothing.
I open my eyes. It all begins.
I am in deep slumber. There is nothing.
The sleep ends, I open my eyes and it all starts.

The eyes represent all my senses. I feel the touch, the smell, and the taste. I sense the movement. Then it begins.

I am in the midst of a vast ocean. I look around. There is no end. All around is awesome endlessness.

Suddenly – far, far away – emerges the horizon. Faint glimmers, elusive glimpses. The closer I move, the further it recedes. Its limitlessness engulfs me. Then the outlines emerge. I make out the coastline and then the shore. Boundaries become discernible. What was limitless becomes limited and bounded.

There is deep darkness. There is nothing.
Is this really so?
Everything is there: men and women, children and the aged, buildings and roads, birds and animals, mountains and oceans. I do not see them. Nor do I notice anything else.

It is all darkness. Utter darkness. There is nothing. Infinite nothingness reigns. All around there is nothing but undifferentiated homogeneity. Darkness swathed in darkness. And then a small lamp is lit. Dim outlines emerge. Outlines become men and women, children and the aged, buildings and roads, birds and animals, mountains and oceans. Slowly, the variety and diversity emerge. The universe comes into being.

Consciousness marks the beginning. Consciousness of existence. Existence of objects. Consciousness of men and women, children and the aged, buildings and roads, birds and animals, mountains and oceans. As if a vacant space has been filled with numerous objects.

Consciousness is like a vast, vacant space. It contains innumerable objects. Every object is in space. Within each object there is space. The room is in space. There is space within the room.

The universe is in consciousness. Consciousness is in the universe. Consciousness is in the cosmos. The cosmos is in consciousness.

Consciousness notices and gives a name.
It detects. A form is etched.
It observes and discerns the functions.

All this – giving a name, drawing a form and noticing the functions – does not happen in that sequence. It occurs almost at the same time. If there is a form, there is a name, and if there is a name and a form, it has a function. This is the triad – name, form and function. The universe comprises innumerable such triads.

Without this triad, consciousness is infinite. When triads emerge, it becomes finite. Name, form and function bring the infinite in the embrace of the finite. Each triad is finite. Altogether, submerged in oneness, they are infinite.

Words are finite and finite words cannot fully express the infinite. So we take recourse to examples. We give illustrations. We attempt to point out an aspect or two. We seek to define.

The infinite, in its totality, is indefinable.

In what does this piece of cloth exist? Does it have an existence other than the thread? If we were to remove all the threads, where would the cloth be? Cloth is a pattern in which the threads are arranged. But for the thread, there would be no pattern. Names and forms and functions make the pattern.

What is there before the names and forms? There is nothing. What is nothingness? We do not know. A state represented by the 'negation' of all-physical attributes? Even less than a vacuum? A vacuum can still possess dimensionality and extension. Nothingness would have no extension, no structure. It is the essential principle which becomes a name, attains a form and gains various functions. It smells. It can be touched. It can be seen. It can be experienced. From nothing emerges something, all things.

There is this vast limitless ocean. Still. Tranquil. Without a ripple. Without any movement. Without even the slightest disturbance. Silent. Quiet. As if it is not there. It is not noticeable. It is not discernible. It is not describable.

Then there is a slight, a very slight disturbance. There is just a bubble. A very tiny bubble. There is a beginning. A delicate beginning. Then another bubble. Then yet another. One bubble clashes with the other. There is more movement. A new entity emerges. The bubbles multiply. Their interfaces continue. New entities emerge. The process continues. Where there was nothing, the cosmos comes into being.

Words are finite and finite words cannot fully express the infinite. Before the words, there is silence. Absolute silence. Unlimited silence. Then there is sound. It surfaces and fades. It is born and then dies. It begins and ends. What was unlimited becomes limited. Infinite becomes finite. There is a beginning and there is an end.

What is there when there is nothing? What is there before the first bubble in the vast limitless oceans? What is there before the first ray pierces the unbounded darkness? What is there before the first triad? What is there before the first finite object emerges? Words are finite and finite words cannot express fully the infinite.

I am finite. I am also the infinite. I close my eyes and look within. There is the vast limitless sky. Innumerable objects float in that firmament. In the limitlessness within my limited being, I travel long distances, meet numerous people, go into the past and run into the future, live in the present. There is infinite within the finite. Remove the finite and there is infinite. Consciousness is the infinite sky. In that blue heaven innumerable finite objects float. Words are finite and finite words cannot fully express the infinite.

I am in deep slumber. There is nothing. I do not exist. There is a slight commotion, a very slight commotion. A tiny bubble in the limitless infinite ocean. I begin to dream. I create a universe. In that universe, I meet friends and enemies. I run and shout. I love and quarrel. I am happy and in pain. I laugh and cry. I become rich and I become destitute. I am on the top of a mountain and I am sailing in a river. There is further disturbance. The dream is shattered. The universe vanishes. There is a beginning. There is the end. There is infinite nothingness before this beginning. There is infinite nothingness after this end. Words are finite and finite words cannot fully express the infinite.

I am born and I grow. I play and I read. I argue and I love. I make friends and enemies. I fly in the air and cruise in the sea. I am happy and I am depressed. I become strong and rich. I become poor and weak. I grow old and I die. There is a beginning and there is an end. What is there before the beginning? What is there before this end?

There is a rhythm in the universe. The planets move regularly. The stars ride their appointed paths. Everywhere, there is the Law of Rhythm. Everything conforms to that law.

Nothingness is zero – *shunya*. It is infinity. Add zero to zero. It remains zero. Subtract zero from zero. It remains zero. Add infinity to infinity. It is infinity. Subtract infinity from infinity. It remains infinity. This infinity becomes finite and marks the beginning. Every finite object ultimately is subsumed in the infinite. It marks the end. A bubble arises in the ocean. It marks the beginning. Bubbles are subsumed in the ocean. It marks the end. For the bubble, the ocean remains as it was. Infinite and still, before the beginning and after the end.

There is a flicker in the eyes and the universe opens up. The eyes close and the universe vanishes. It is there before the eyes open. It is there after the eyes close. I am born and my universe begins. I die and my universe ends. It is there before I am born and it is there after I die.

There is a beginning and there is an end. There is something before the beginning and something after the end. There is infinity before the finite and there is infinity after the finite.

This is Truth. This is Reality. This is the limitless ocean – still and tranquil. This is Brahma.
Brahma desires. It is *mana.*
Mana moves. This is prana.
The first bubble emerges. This is *wak*.
This is the silence before the first sound.
This silence is bliss. Infinite bliss.
We experience infinity as *sat*, *chit* and ananda: Truth, Consciousness and Bliss.

Before the beginning, there is nothing. 'Nothing' is the negation of physical entities. It is the universe of supraphysical energies. These are the first stirrings. They come into motion spontaneously. They cause the beginning (of the physical universe). After the end (of the physical universe), they subsume everything. The waves arise in the ocean. This marks the beginning. The waves vanish in the ocean. This marks the end. There is ocean before the beginning. There is ocean after the end.

The *rishis* tell us what is there before the beginning. They tell us what is after the end. They tell us that there is no beginning and there is no end. They take us into the supraphysical universe. They help us float in that limitless sky within us. They bless us with that little light (of knowledge) which causes the flicker that opens our eyes. They guide us into the world of light.

I go back in time, to the beginning. The whole universe is reduced to a speck. Matter, energy and space disappear. With the vanishing of these three, time also disappears. There is neither a beginning nor an end.

Words are finite and finite words cannot fully express the infinite. But consciousness is infinite. Therefore, she can experience the infinite. How do I communicate this encounter? I etch the happening as 'Vishnu'. Resting in the midst of an ocean (infinity), lying on the bed of a coiled serpent (the frightening turbulence of the physical universe) with his consort Lakshmi by his side (the female complementarity).

I sketch consciousness as an enthralling goddess, a finite figure on the limitless canvas of infinity. A sculptor carves her in stone. A painter draws her on the walls of a cave. These are efforts to convey the incommunicable. Ecstasy captured in a poem. Infinity secured in finiteness. The limitless sky caged within the confines of my mind. Indescribable beauty imprisoned in an image.

Love expressed in silence.

NOTES

1. Readers are encouraged to read more deeply on this topic in Chapter Six, 'Who is the "I"?', in RK Mishra's first volume in this series entitled *Before the Beginning and After the End*, 2000, pp.117 – 128.
2. Please see Chapter Seven, 'The Universe: Inside and Outside' in RK Mishra's *Before the Beginning and After the End* for a more detailed analysis of the relationship between our physical form and the universe.
3. For a detailed study of prana, please refer to 'Section 3: Energy' in *The Realm of Supraphysics: Mind, Energy and Matter in the Light of the* Vedas by RK Mishra, 2003, pp. 119 – 144.

SECTION FOUR

~

WHOLENESS IN KASHMIRI SHAIVISM

Chapter 6

INTRODUCTION

Kashmiri Shaivism is one of the major vibrant schools of eastern *darshana*. Its world view is a creative blend of monistic, theistic and logical thought construct. Like yoga, it combines a practical regimen with a rigorous and internally consistent analysis of the totality and wholeness of the universe.

Kashmiri Shaivism draws its name from Shiva, the ultimate all-pervasive reality principle which manifests in the form of five energies – these being the energies of consciousness, will, knowledge, action and bliss. Shiva is the fundamental reality underpinning the entire universe. Shakti, the active principle, and Shiva, the fundamental reality or Absolute, are one and the same. Absolute reality polarises into static consciousness and the dynamic power of consciousness; together these two constitute universal consciousness.

The entity known as Shiva is really consciousness or Self, and can be considered on a surface level or more deeply. On the surface it is imperfect and limited, while at the deeper level it is perfect and infinite. We can think of the surface as the 'lower' self or 'I', and the deeper aspect as the 'higher' self or 'I'. Thus, we can think of Shiva as 'myself' (of course, my higher self). The question, 'Who am I?', or 'What is my real nature?' ultimately leads to the realisation that our real or deep nature is Shiva, which is also known as Brahman. In describing the nature of Shiva we are, in fact, describing the nature of our real self, and vice versa.

When the word 'Shiva' is used to denote a substance or entity, this includes the lower self, which is individual consciousness. But when used to denote its pure and cosmic form, Shiva excludes all limitations. Let us take the analogy of the ocean and the waves. From the point of view of the substance the wave is nothing but water, as is the ocean. In this sense, the wave can be considered to be the ocean itself. But since the wave is limited and the ocean is a limitless expansion of water, the word 'ocean' may also exclude the waves.

Shiva's nature is the pure light of consciousness (*prakasha*), and it is only through this light of consciousness that things exist. Shakti is the self-reflection of that pure light. Without this self-reflection, there could be no existence and no creation.

These two fundamental principles pass through a series of transformations, as the process of unfolding or emanation continues in nature. Nature itself evolves in various forms. In its original state, it is described as root nature, from which emerge, successively, the intellect and mind, sense powers, subtle matter and, finally, the gross material elements. These are stages of universal consciousness, in which the conscious subject or 'I' is experienced as being identical with Shiva (the Absolute). The object of consciousness is Shakti, which manifests in the form of the entire cosmos.

The statement that Shiva is the Absolute indicates that he is independent. He exists and is sustained by himself, requiring nothing else as a support. This is also known as ultimate reality, and can be contrasted with the term 'relative', which denotes all those phenomena which depend upon some other or others for their existence. Our world is 'relative', for it depends upon Shiva both for its existence and for its sustenance.

The secondary meaning of the term 'Absolute' is that which covers or pervades all. Everything in existence can be called Shiva, for everything in the universe is the self-manifestation or extension of Shiva. This includes consciousness, for awareness or knowledge is the very nature of Shiva, and Shiva is self-illuminating consciousness.

In this section we shall be exploring the various dimensions of Shiva – particularly the nature of consciousness – within the concept of wholeness as understood by Kashmiri Shaivism.[1]

Chapter 7

UNIVERSE: THE ALL-ENCOMPASSING UNITY

As was mentioned in the previous chapter, universal consciousness is Shiva. He is the cause of the universe and thus everything depends on him. Shiva is the transcendent, everlasting, vibratory principle, the Absolute, ultimate reality. He is eternal, pervasive and formless, the activator of everything.

Only consciousness is capable of creating the cosmos, and only consciousness can be the material from which that cosmos is made. Consciousness has its own existence within the silence of the heart. Consciousness is free from the boundaries created by the principles that govern time and the natural order of space and form, cause and effect. In other words, the entire gamut of possibilities and variations of the events and in living beings of the universe is 'happening' in consciousness simultaneously.

The nature of consciousness is to be ready to know, to know and to make known. It does not change, even while it manifests as space, time and form. Consciousness is within the heart, and this individualised consciousness is no different from universal consciousness. We look at this relationship in the following chapter. Consciousness fills all objects, perceptions and activities, while itself remaining free. The knower, the known and the act of knowing are seen as the triad of knowledge, and together they form the fundamental structure of any creation. Right knowledge is the direct awareness of the pervasiveness of consciousness within an individual and outside it. The subject is the light that illuminates, the object is that which is illuminated, and the relationship between them is a function of the illuminative power of knowledge itself.

The light of universal consciousness manifests in individuals as individualised consciousness or the self. This self unfolds its countless powers when it sets out to create a universe and manifests as the subject (perceiver) and the object (perceived). Although the cosmos contains the twofold division of seer and seen, it is always whole, a unity, since there is not a single object in it that cannot be apprehended or illuminated by consciousness. In fact, the universe is made up of the seer and the seen, the perceiver and the perceived. We and the universe are one and the same. We are both supreme consciousness.

Beholding Shiva Face-to-Face

If we want to understand the highest reality we must first understand ourselves, for we are our own doorway to reality. It is only through our own consciousness that we can know supreme consciousness. The universe arises as a pulse of reality and abides in it. It emanates as rays of energy (shakti) in total freedom. Shakti represents the primordial energy, supreme will and absolute ecstasy, and she is the power of consciousness. Metaphorically, one could say that Shakti is the mirror in which Shiva sees himself and exclaims with delight, 'I am!'. In addition to being self-consciousness, she is the creative energy. In conclusion, we exist because we are Shiva; and we are aware of ourself and our world because we are Shakti.

The self is a fact of everybody's direct experience. To realise the self is to 'discover' or 'reclaim' that which already lies within us. The self 'wears' a physical body in much the same way as we wear a suit of clothing. In forgetting our real identity, instead we identify with the suit of clothing – the superficial and relative appearance of our existence including our body, gender, name, skills and idiosyncrasies. But when we come to recognise or remember our most profound identity – our identity with the supreme self – we gain the highest knowledge and direct experience of the self. This recognition inevitably transforms the way in which we view ourselves and the world, and changes our habit of judging ourselves and others based on appearances. It can remove the doubts and patterns of behaviour which cause us to run around in the same circle again and again.

Not a single thought wave can arise separately from universal consciousness. When we become aware of this, we behold Shiva face-to-face. The light of universal consciousness emanates from the centre of our being, like a wave arising in the ocean, and flows in surges of delight through all our senses to capture impressions of the world. That same light then brings those impressions inward and, through the agency of the mind, leaves them as offerings for the enjoyment of the luminous self.

Just as the sun's rays flow spontaneously from the orb of the sun, so does the universe in its infinite entirety spontaneously manifest from universal consciousness. And the natural and spontaneous activities of universal consciousness give rise to forms, which arise from, are sustained by, and dissolve into universal consciousness. We can compare this to professional actors who assume different roles and appearances, yet understand that each character they play is equally their own creation.

The inner consciousness is the self; and our inner states of contradiction or expansion, joy or sorrow, anxiety or ignorance and so forth are all reactions to outer stimuli. Yet whatever we experience in the three states of waking, dreaming and deep sleep simply manifests in one of these three phases of the same supreme state, and the bliss of this state can be enjoyed in all three. The self is the witness of the waking, dreaming and deep sleep states. In the waking state, the self functions in the gross body and experiences gross objects with the five organs of perception, the five organs of action, the five forms of prana and the fourfold psychic instrument. In dreams, the self experiences a more subtle realm; and in deep sleep, it experiences the joy that accompanies the dreamless state of rest. The relationship of the senses and the sense objects is this: while the senses perceive, delight in and act on their respective objects, Shiva is the experience and Shiva is also that which is experienced.

Knowledge is wakefulness. The state of waking when coupled with ignorance is darkness. But when we have evolved from the state of ignorance to the state of full knowledge, we become truly awake. A person whose eye of knowledge is opened becomes transmuted into pure consciousness. Such a person can see the 'nature' of a pot as clay without having to break the pot into pieces to prove its existence as clay. In the same way, we should cultivate the awareness of the self as the universe, without feeling that we need to discard the universe or run away from it in order to penetrate reality.

The universe made of consciousness is consciousness, in the same way as pots made from clay are still clay, and ornaments beaten out of gold are still gold, and cloth woven from thread is still thread. The phantasmagoria of innumerable thoughts and fancies is nothing but the mind. Gaining this true insight, the mind becomes tranquil. An ocean may be serene even while holding rocks, mountains, trees and gigantic creatures in its depths. Similarly, universal consciousness remains serene while holding the cosmos within itself.

Knowledge of the Self

Truth is realised when the intellect understands and truly 'knows' the unity within the universe. At this level of deep realisation, even the subtlest stirrings of the self are realised. The continuing awareness of the universe as an unfolding of self refines the intellect and establishes oneness with the self.

Self beholds the same light within and without, permeating its gross and subtle bodies. The light of the self spreads through the whole universe. The entire cosmos possesses the same reality that is within the self. *Here* is the body, prana, senses and mind, and *there* is where the outer universe is. All things and all beings embody the same impalpable essence.

In effect, this entire universe is the 'sport' of universal consciousness. Consciousness becomes unity, diversity, and unity in diversity. It reveals the world. The heat of fire and its power to burn are no different from the fire itself. Similarly, the power of universal consciousness is no different from the supreme principle. It is self-effulgent, just as a flame illuminates both itself and all around it, or as the sun illuminates both itself and this entire world. We do not need a second flame to see the flame, nor do we need another sun to see the sun. Similarly, consciousness illuminates and comprehends itself with its own knowledge.

As individuals, we possess the freedom to establish a universe in which we can live blissfully. Recognising this potential gives us access to a part of our nature that is innate, although often forgotten. However, it is necessary to underline the fact that personal freedom is the capacity to want what we have – to experience joy in the face of any circumstance, and thus to exercise our own will to choose.

Creating our own Universe

The term 'individual' means 'a particular being' with a name, form and function. This is what distinguishes each of us as a separate, experiencing entity. The act of my 'knowing' in this way is crucial in giving personal meaning to everything around me. Without this capacity, 'I' would not be an individual at all; 'I' would be in the Great Void.

Having taken the form of an individual, consciousness chooses to forget, at least partially, her attributes of omnipotence, omniscience and rapturous fullness, of eternality, freedom and all-pervasiveness. It is as if a creative force wraps itself around the individual self. We become limited by our lack of understanding of our own true nature, and we dwell only on the superficial 'level' of thought. It is our thoughts that make up our world. When we become aware of the way our mind thinks, the way our intellect judges, the way our ego parades around, of the way our subconscious mind retains all the impressions of our thoughts and actions – then we come to understand the necessity of self-realisation and search for ways to attain it.

It is the ego that connects us to the world 'out there'. Through experience, ego creates the notion of 'I'. Ego overlooks the fact that what we perceive as being 'out there' is actually a projection appearing on our inner screen (*buddhi*), and the understandings we have about that projection come from our own memory.

However, when we understand the nature of the self, our intellect becomes 'clean' and, like a mirror, reflects all phenomena perfectly. While we cannot control all the events that occur in our life, we can take responsibility for what we perceive, how we understand our perceptions and the behaviour which that understanding inspires. As individuals we are responsible for creating our own universe and we are able to do so when we comprehend the all-encompassing unity underlying the variegated diversity.

Chapter 8

CONSCIOUSNESS: INDIVIDUAL AND UNIVERSAL

Consciousness is universal. However, its universality does not remain as the homogenous source of the universe alone, for it also manifests as individual consciousness. In other words, universal consciousness in its limited state manifests in individuals. Kashmiri Shaivism explores this interface and helps us understand the relationship between the two. It also reveals the process by which we, endowed with individualised consciousness, can connect with universal consciousness.

In this chapter we trace the journey from limited consciousness to universal consciousness. To travel thus, we need to remove the impurities that obstruct the light of consciousness. These impurities, or defects, are caused when we falsely identify ourself as a limited being rather than the reality, which is that we are identical with the source of unlimited consciousness (Shiva). This amounts to denial of our inherent freedom, and in this way we lose the power of independence which is integral to universal consciousness.

This loss of freedom is bondage and is caused by our limited knowledge, which fetters our consciousness at the level of the gross material elements of earth, water, air, fire and space. The self – which in reality is all-pervasive – becomes interlocked with, and constricted by, the intellect. Traces of pleasure and pain, as the consequences of our past actions, give rise to further impurities or defects.

The state of individual consciousness is manifest in every individual, and is also manifest in the body, breath and intellect. The process is as follows: thinking takes place in our intellect, which exists in our consciousness; and individualised consciousness exists in the state of supreme universal consciousness. Nothing exists separately from consciousness.

The self is a vacuum filled with consciousness, within which are to be found a whole spectrum of states, ranging from unlimited universal consciousness to limited individualised consciousness. To experience this entire spectrum, we need to concentrate on the totality of both aspects of consciousness. Self captures the substratum of all entities and proximates the term *atma*, which shines through the interval between two successive states of consciousness. Normally we are not able to experience it, because the energy that propels us from one experience to another moves at such a great speed that this interval continues to elude us. However, through the practice of introspective meditation, it is possible to sense these fleeting intervals between two consecutive states of consciousness, when the supreme light flashes forth. In those moments we experience universal unconditioned consciousness, and we are endowed with the energy of will that enables us to become master of our self.

The other way of experiencing consciousness is the attainment of knowledge through the means of mantra. The word 'mantra' is made up of the two syllables of *man* and *tra*. 'Man' from the word *manan* means '[that which] causes you to reside in your own consciousness'. 'Tra' from the word *trana* means '[that which] protects you from all evils of the world'[2]. Mantras embody energies, visualised as a female entity, which are latent in us like a sleeping serpent coiled around the spark of light concealed in our heart. Concentration on this spark arouses her and the coiled one becomes straight. When she is mastered, we attain an enormous increase in our intellectual power and a limited bliss. (We explore mantra in the context of the power of words in the chapter 'Sound and Communication' later in this work.)

The Power of Cognition

As noted earlier, this universe is a world of consciousness, and supreme consciousness is the ultimate reality. An individual who has not come into consciousness does not exist at all. Consciousness is a unique reality of supreme movement, a vibration in an inexhaustible, limitless ocean of energy. The common characteristic of all objects is that they are manifested by the one who cognises them. That which is not cognised has no existence; a thing can be properly said to exist only when it is cognised by a conscious being. Thus, cognition endows it with existential value, as it is the manifestation of that which was previously unmanifest. Cognition is a self-determined activity, unlimited by anything outside itself. In other words, the power of cognition is characterised by independence or self-determination.

This universe includes everything: whatever we feel, whatever we hear, whatever we experience in the daily routine of life. All of this forms part of the universal dance,[3] which displays continuous movement. Shiva is the embodiment of movement, and hence there is movement in everything, down to the tiniest blade of grass. And not only in a minute blade of grass, for there is movement also in a rock. Rocks seem to us to be absolutely dead, without life. But there is life in a rock – which is why, over time, it undergoes change.

As the manifestation of energy, this universe has two dimensions: energy and the energy holder. The energy holder is Shiva himself, from whom arise five energies: the energies of consciousness, bliss, will, knowledge and action. These encompass three fundamental energies from which the power of freedom of universal consciousness arises: the energy of will, knowledge and action. All these energies flow outward from the centre, which is universal consciousness.

To experience and internalise the complete freedom and unfettered independence of universal consciousness is the paramount goal of human life. This freedom flows from a correct understanding, which is not conferred by any external source but is a function of our own will. It is entirely up to us to choose whether we wish to bind ourselves or to free ourselves. Both possibilities are under our control. This freedom is experienced when we recognise our connection with the ultimate source of all energies that float in the universe.

A state of ignorance of the undifferentiated nature of universal consciousness, blinkered by perceived differences, constitutes impurity and makes our understanding defective. Impurity is ignorance and ignorance leads to bondage. The symptom of bondage is the feeling that we are incomplete. When ego dominates, the universal 'I' is limited within the individualised 'I'. The latter is limited by the mind, the organs of knowledge, the organs of action and the gross material elements. Impurity flows from limited action and limited knowledge. Universal consciousness is lost when our understanding is clouded by these impurities. They arise out of our attachment to the three internal organs of the mind, intellect and ego.

Shiva and Shakti: Energy and the World

This universe, filled with infinite diversity, is neither different nor separate from the supreme light of consciousness known as Shiva. The external objective world is nothing but the expansion of his energy (Shakti), filled with the glorious radiance of universal consciousness. In this sense, Shiva is the energy holder, and the universal state of the objective field is his energy or power, which is known as Shakti.[4] When this energy expands, objective impressions arise and the universe comes into being. When it contracts, the dissolution of those impressions takes place. The expansion of energy manifests as impressions of the objective world in our mind.

If for the sake of convenience we were to make a distinction between Shakti and Shiva, then we could say that Shakti is this whole universe, and that from which this universe issues forth is Shiva. Yet in reality these two are one and the same, just as fire is one with heat. The universe is a reflection of Shiva. It is not created in the same way as a woman creates a child, who at birth becomes separate from her. Rather, this universe is created in the same way as the image of an object is reflected in a mirror. However, in the case of Shiva there is no object or entity which exists independently of the mirror, for the only thing that exists is the object seen in the mirror.

The way to recognise the source of universal consciousness (Shiva) is not by abandoning the universe but by observing and experiencing universal consciousness in the very activities of the world. Attempting to realise universal consciousness by cutting ourselves off from the universe will take an inordinately long time; whereas those who remain engaged in worldly activities while being attentive to realising consciousness will attain it very easily. The light of a candle is outshone by the light of the sun; but the radiance of the sun's light is neither outshone by an external light nor overshadowed by darkness. This is because both external light and darkness reside in the supreme light of consciousness, like the sun. This external universe is the very means by which we can realise our own nature.

Two Levels of Consciousness

People are sometimes intimidated by the independent free will of Shiva. This is because of their ignorance. They do not know of his existence, and they do not even feel that they are ignorant. If they did feel that they did not know, they would know. According to Kashmiri Shaivism, we are Shiva. As we overcome our ignorance we come to recognise the truth that we are Shiva. Until we gain that recognition, however, in one sense we are not actually Shiva because we have not attained that understanding.

This entire universe is filled with the knowledge of universal consciousness. No one has ever perceived an object without this knowledge, which takes the form of the object. Thus objective knowledge is not separate from the knowledge of universal consciousness, for the former takes place by means of the latter. These two levels of consciousness need to unite in order for knowledge to occur. When we simultaneously possess this unity of objective and universal knowledge, that which is known becomes knowledge and knowledge becomes the known object, and both knowledge and the knower are filled with enlightenment. We can become enlightened completely either by knowledge or the knower which are, in the ultimate sense, one. Every person has the power of knowing and acting accordingly.

Earlier in this work we began to explore three states of experience: waking, dreaming and deep sleep. These three states of consciousness are one with the fourth state, which is called *tureeya*. This is an expansive state which is held in the consciousness during the differentiated states of waking, dreaming and deep sleep. The three states of waking, dreaming and deep sleep are nothing more nor less than the all-pervasive expansion of universal consciousness. If this threefold world did not exist in universal consciousness, the impressions in each different state would not arise.

For example, we enter the dreaming state, then we enter the dreamless state, and then after some time we wake up; throughout these three states, universal consciousness exists. Between each of these states there is a gap, a point where one state ceases to exist and the next state has yet to begin. If we direct our consciousness we find that point or gap when our consciousness, having left one world, has not yet entered the next. We are able to travel through that gap because universal consciousness exists in it. Although we usually perceive the objective world as being separate from the subjective world, in actual fact universal consciousness maintains the continuity of awareness and memory in all states. For someone who enjoys the unity of awareness of all three states, this entire perceived world is encompassed within the self.

The Supreme State

In the normal mind, thoughts flicker constantly. Yet it is possible to settle and focus the mind through the practice of one-pointedness. Adepts in this practice are able to discard the differentiation of objectivity and subjectivity, aided by their practice of meditation. The power of the supreme 'I' is attained by the attentive continuity of meditation on the great ocean of consciousness. According to Kashmiri Shaivism, the universe is created by this supreme energy of consciousness through the interaction of the energy of will with the energy of action. By this fusion, that which is willed occurs at once. Intensive practitioners who aim the energy of their will completely from the core of their heart – not as an afterthought or superfluously – are able to achieve whatever they desire.

Awareness needs to be developed in order to realise this state. The more we develop awareness, the closer we come to universal consciousness; for it is our own ignorance that brings about the absence of awareness. If we use the energy of our will, such absence of awareness will not occur. For those who are fully aware of universal consciousness, all the organs of cognition and of action and the internal organs converge in the supreme state of universal consciousness. Those who are not aware of this are deprived of this connection by the same organs. Several currents continue to rise in supreme consciousness, such as the currents of sound, touch, smell and so on. Universal consciousness is like a great ocean, absolutely pure and transparent, unlimited in depth. Nothing can stop its flow.

One who is aware of the connection of self with universal consciousness is the actor in this universal drama, while those who are unaware of this connection are manipulated like puppets. Experiencing sadness, joy, depression and other emotions, they are unable to transcend these experiences because they are continuously manipulated by mind, intellect and ego, and by their own delusions. They fall into two categories: those who are capable of taking initiative and those who are incapable of doing so.

Freedom of Consciousness

We are all aware of dual actions such as inhaling and exhaling. Awareness of the two is the awareness of dialectic actions. There is also a third dimension, and the three together constitute the triple consciousness which includes the junction or gap between any two actions, such as between inhaling and exhaling. This junction occurs between one step and another, between one thought and another, between one sensation and another, and so on. When we are cognisant of all three centres of awareness, we are transported to universal consciousness where differentiated perceptions cease to exist. When we rest our consciousness in the three states of awareness, we become one with universal consciousness.

Individualised consciousness relates to the state of being wherein the awareness exists that 'I' am the body, 'I' am the sense organs and organs of action, 'I' am the mind, the intellect and the ego. This state (*jeeva*) manifests as individualised consciousness, and is alleviated when our consciousness shines in its own nature. Upon returning from the state of universal consciousness to the state of individualised consciousness, the connection with inhaling and exhaling occurs naturally. It is Shiva's nature to travel with the movement of the breath; as soon as he descends from the state of universal consciousness he begins his journey of inhaling and exhaling.

According to Kashmiri Shaivism, every individual is endowed with the power of creation. This is confirmed by the experience of dreaming and imagination. In such states we have the power to create and destroy as we will. For example, in our dreams we may create a car, the road to drive on and the landscape to drive through – in other words, we create an entire universe. This power of creation is experienced by every individual. In the world of imagination and of dreaming we can create a world that we are unable to create when awake.

But when we secure and strengthen the power of our awareness, we can develop the power to 'create' in the waking state also, and our desire becomes just like a wish-fulfilling tree. The essence of this power of doing and of undoing is the manifestation of the freedom of universal consciousness. The realisation of this power of absolute freedom carries us to that supreme summit of experience.

With sustained practice, and following the processes laid down in Kashmiri Shaivism, we can become an adept. When we desire something with an intense force of awareness, that desire comes true not only in the dreaming state or world of imagination but also in the waking state. We can also create worlds of our own in the waking state. In fact, we can create whatever we desire in the outside world, and these worlds which we have created can also be perceived by others.

Chapter 9

FLAVOUR OF ONENESS

As noted in the previous chapter, ignorance is the failure to experience directly the intimate connection between the infinite and the finite. The finite is a symbol of the infinite, and the latter stamps its seal (*mudra*) onto its own nature replete with all possible forms of the finite.

Thus, reality is constant in the midst of change. What this means essentially is that there is change although nothing changes.[5] The impossible situation is reflected in the ultimate impossibility of change itself. That which does not exist prior to its changing and does not exist after it has changed must be equally non-existent between these two moments.

Just as everything that falls into a salt mine becomes salty, so all diversity grounded in unity shares the single flavour of oneness.[6] Undeniably there are differences between individual phenomena; but the distinction we perceive between two entities, which leads us to think that one differs from the other, is merely external. Such relative distinction is not an inherent quality of things signifying that they can divide their innate nature. This is not because this division is in any way unreal but because it operates within the domain of the real, which appears as phenomenally manifest entities and is based on the difference between their manifest forms.

Thus the relative distinction between two realities or *tattwa*s[7] is not impossible. This is the doctrine of supreme unity in which relative distinction is neither shunned nor accepted. While there is (an external) difference between phenomena, there is none (inwardly), established as they are in their own essential nature.[8]

Reality is one, which becomes manifest as many. Universal being moves between two poles – that is, between the diversification of the one and the unification of the many.[9] Thought interferes with our direct intuitive understanding of this fact, dividing the two aspects of this movement into separate categories. Reality is a structured whole, consisting of a graded hierarchy of metaphysical principles corresponding to the planes of existence. On the lowest planes up to the level of ignorance or delusion (*maya*), we experience division between objects and ourselves. At the highest level, we reach the plane of unity which pervades and contains within itself all the others.

All the categories of existence are present in every single category. The yogi experiences every individual particular as the sum total of everything else, recognising that all things have one nature and that every particular is all things. This is the essence or co-extensive unity of all things.[10]

Reality is pure consciousness alone (*samvid*), and consciousness and being are synonymous.[11] Reality is the point where the intelligible and the sensible meet in the common unity of being; it cannot be said to exist in itself outside of or apart from knowledge or vision. The universe and consciousness are two aspects of the whole, just as quality and substance constitute two aspects of a single entity. The universe is an attribute (*dharma*) of consciousness, which bears it (*dharmin*) as its substance.

Consciousness is more than the awareness individuals have of themselves and their environment. It is an eternal, all-pervasive principle, the highest reality, and all things are a manifestation of it.[12] The essential nature of this pure universal consciousness is the true nature of the self.

Rather than being a passive witness, consciousness is full of the conscious activity through which it generates the universe and reabsorbs it into itself at the end of each cycle of creation. The freedom of consciousness to do this is its sovereign power. The vibration of consciousness is both dynamic and creative. Kashmiri Shaivism calls it 'the divine power' (*spanda*).[13] The vibration of the energy of consciousness engages in the act of perception and manifests externally as its own object. When the act of perception is complete, consciousness reabsorbs the object and resumes its undifferentiated inner nature. All matter in the entire universe is absolutely real, existing as 'condensed' or 'contracted' forms of consciousness.[14]

Vibration is the spontaneous and recurrent pulsation of the Absolute, which objectively manifests as the rhythm of the arising and subsidence of every detail of the cosmic picture appearing within its infinite expanse. At the same time, it is the inner universal vibration of consciousness as pure perceptivity, which constitutes equally its cognising subjectivity and agency. The Absolute is both universal consciousness and humankind's authentic nature (*atman*).

Just as boiled sugarcane juice condenses to form treacle, brown sugar, sugar and candy, all of which retain the sweetness of the sugarcane, similarly consciousness abides unchanged even while assuming the concrete material form of the five gross elements. The same reality thus abides equally in gross and subtle forms, and consequently no object is totally insentient. As noted earlier, even inanimate objects like stones bear a trace of consciousness, although it is not clearly apparent because it is not associated with the vital breath (prana) and other components of a psycho-physical organism.[15]

The inscrutable pulse of consciousness moves and yet moves not, changes and yet remains eternally itself. It ensures that both manifestation and the Absolute (its unmanifest source) form part of a single process, which passes freely from one to the other in such a way that both poles are at the same level and equally real.[16] The content of absolute consciousness consists of diverse appearances which, because they are manifest through it in this way, do not compromise the wholeness of consciousness.

The Light of Consciousness

Light and awareness are the two aspects of consciousness. The divine light of consciousness and the reflective awareness this light has of its own nature together constitute the all-embracing fullness of consciousness. Prakasha is the pure 'luminosity' or self-showing that constitutes the essence and ultimate identity (atman) of phenomena. That things appear at all is due to the light which bestows on them their evident, manifest nature. Established in the light of consciousness, everything appears there according to its own specific nature. This light is the conjunction or unity of its countless manifest forms and the collective whole of all the categories of existence. The universe is nothing other than the shining of the light within itself. It is the radiant vibration of this light, the state in which consciousness becomes manifest.

This light is the highest reality. It makes all things new and fresh every moment. It is the form of the present, the eternal 'now'. Time and space are in relationship to the contents of consciousness; they cannot impinge on the integrity of the Absolute itself.[17] Nothing shines – that is, appears, manifests or exists in its apparent form – unless illuminated by the light of consciousness.

If the light of consciousness were devoid of reflective awareness it would be as inert and lifeless as the light of a crystal.[18] In contrast, the light of consciousness not only illuminates and makes manifest all things but it is a living light which reflects on itself in an infinite self-conscious subjectivity. This subjectivity, as the pure 'I' sense, is the very 'life' of all living beings. Light represents consciousness as its own illuminating knowledge and awareness as its activity.

The most profoundly satisfying experience possible is the recognition that the light of one's own consciousness is all things. This bliss is unlike the intoxication of wine or of riches or of union with the beloved. It is unlike the rays of light emanating from a lamp, the sun or the moon. When one frees oneself from accumulated multiplicity, the state of bliss is like putting down a burden one has been carrying for so long. The manifestation of the light within is like acquiring a lost treasure – the domain of universal non-duality.

The dynamic character of the light of consciousness is represented by the flux of cognition. This is the pulsation of its noetic activity, of which it is itself the conscious agent as well as the perceiver. As we discuss elsewhere in more detail, knowledge cannot exist independently of the knower. The object is grounded in knowledge and knowledge in the subject, which thus binds them together like a powerful adhesive. Ultimately these three are identical: nothing perceived is independent of perception, and perception does not differ from the perceiver. Therefore, the universe is nothing but the perceiver oneself.[19] Thus the one universal consciousness has three aspects: it is the illuminator, the illuminated universe, and the light of knowledge which illuminates it. To put it another way, the universe, light and self are one. Subject, object and means of knowledge necessarily attend each act of perception and make cognitive awareness (*prama*) possible.

The group of subjects, the various means of knowledge, the multiple kinds of knowledge and the objects of knowledge – all of these are consciousness alone. The absolute freedom of our own consciousness assumes these various forms. The creativity of consciousness consists in its diversification in many modes having apparent externality; it is not a creation of objects. The forms are aspects of dynamic consciousness, which is Shiva's freedom to act as the agent of cognition. They are phases of his vibration. This movement of conscious energy, incandescent with the light of consciousness, generates cognitions that appear as manifestations of consciousness.

Consciousness is the ultimate principle of revelation. The light of consciousness reveals everything without requiring a second light for its own revelation. If consciousness were not 'self conscious' but required another consciousness to reveal its nature, that too would require another and the third a fourth, and so on ad infinitum.[20]

Like a mirror, consciousness can reflect objects within itself. It has the power to manifest entities that are separate from it as if they were one with it, without in any way affecting its nature. Conversely, it also makes manifest these reflected images as if they were distinct from it, although they are not. Even while various manifest forms appear to be separate from one another, this does not compromise the oneness of consciousness.

However, the mirror is a limited analogy for consciousness, because from the point of view of consciousness the original object is as much a reflection as the image reflected in the mirror. Although the universe is like a reflection, there is no object outside the mirror of consciousness that, reflected within it, appears as the universe. The image reflected in a mirror is deposited there by the original external object. Now, if this too is a reflected image, what remains of the original object?

The formless, pervasive nature of consciousness makes it possible for objects to be related to each other, and we do in fact experience a variety of objects in a single act of perception. This is only possible because the light of consciousness is fundamentally one and the same for each object. The light which illuminates them is both formless and omniform at the same time.[21]

The Ultimate Experience of Reality

Consciousness is the direct perception of entities just as they are in themselves, insofar as it is experience-as-such, free of thought constructs. Moreover, objects are not momentary. A conscious self must persist unchanged in order to connect a previous perception with a subsequent perception as a necessary condition for recognition.[22] Thus a unity must exist between the perception of a previously perceived object and its recollection in order that its recognition as the same be possible.

In the Kashmiri Shaivism tradition, Bhairava is understood as the divine form of the Absolute, realised as the exertive force that drives the senses and mind at the microcosmic level and the universe at the macrocosmic level.[23] Through an inner process of realisation we discover our essential identity with the flow of the power of consciousness. This occurs through the polarities of subject, object and means of knowledge, in consonance with their arising and falling away in each act of perception. Liberation is essentially freedom from the opposites of good and evil; thus the adept who seeks it must break through to a higher state of expanded and blissful consciousness which, unaffected by these perceived polar opposites, encompasses both. Liberating knowledge is gained not by going beyond appearances but by attending closely to them.

The ultimate experience is this realisation that everything is contained within consciousness. We can discover this in two ways: either we merge the external world into the inner subject, or we look upon the outer as a gross form of the inner. In one of these two ways we come to recognise that all things reside within our own consciousness, just as consciousness resides within them. This all-embracing inwardness is possible if there is an essential identity between the universe and consciousness.

When we are blinded by ignorance or delusion (maya) and bound by our actions (karma), we are fettered to the endless rounds of birth and death. We fail to recognise our identity with Shiva, the one reality who is the life and being of every existing thing. Instead, we perceive only our individual identity, and this delusion severs us from one another and from ourself. For this reason we appear to be sullied by our actions and afflicted by the myriad conditions that stand as obstacles to the realisation of our goal.

But when we recognise our true universal nature, our divine sovereignty and power filled with consciousness alone, we become liberated and attain the ultimate goal of life. Realising that everything is a part of ourself, extending our being in wonderfully diverse forms, we achieve true recognition of reality and, with it, the conviction that we are not in fact a slave of creation (*pasu*) but of its master (*pati*). In this way, we discover our spiritual power. The ultimate experience of enlightenment consists of a profound and irreversible recognition that our own authentic identity is Shiva himself.

When perfection is achieved in both movements – that is, from the finite to the infinite and back – we participate in the universal vibration of the Absolute and share in its essential freedom. Thenceforth, we no longer travel 'to' and 'from' but eternally 'through' the Absolute, which is realised to be at once infinite and finite.

Absolute being is not an existing quality to be found in things, nor is it an object of thought or the result of production. It is that from which both speech and mind turn back, unable to comprehend its fullness. To make this point, Shankara quotes a passage from a lost *Upanishad* in his commentary on the *Brahmasutra*. Baskali, an Upanishadic sage, is being questioned by his disciple about the nature of the Absolute. He sits motionless and silent. 'Teach me, sir!' prays the disciple earnestly several times, but the teacher maintains his silence. Finally, he answers his student thus: 'I am teaching, but you do not understand. The self *is* silence.'[24]

Chapter 10

INDIVIDUALS AND INFINITY: THE ROLE OF MIND

All individuals arise from an infinite, limitless and tranquil ocean of supraphysical energy. To remind our readers, an individual is a person, object or entity which is endowed with a name, form and function. The process of evolution of an individual from an ocean of infinity is subtle and somewhat spontaneous. Within that ocean of supraphysical energy there is a stir; suddenly, a tiny bubble becomes discernible. This very slight disturbance in the equilibrium is sustained by the tranquillity of the ocean; it is like the rise of a wave on the surface of the ocean. Then innumerable such bubbles begin to float on the surface of the ocean, and innumerable waves begin to rise and fall. Each of these bubbles and waves is distinct in itself while at the same time comprising a tiny part of a comprehensive whole.

This distinction between a bubble and a wave, and between waves and the ocean, is apparent and superficial, for the wholeness is real and enduring. In reality, it is like the space in a jar, the space in a room and the space in a small hole – all of these are integral parts of one cosmic space. In fact, they are all various facets of infinite space in which there are no parts. And, like the waves that arise in the ocean and merge with it, these individuals also arise and are subsumed in the infinite ocean of supraphysical energy.

The first bubble that appears is a manifestation of the power of will of the infinite. The infinite is the ocean of supreme consciousness known as Shiva, who is the source of this universe and whose playground is the universe. The infinite appears to be the doer, and the rise of the bubble his action; but in fact, the action and the doer of the action manifest spontaneously at the same time, in the same way as a flower and its fragrance concurrently exist.

As noted in a previous chapter, it is simply our ignorance that prevents us from recognising this interconnectedness of individuals and infinity. Our ignorance leads us to see the rise and dissolution of waves in the ocean and the ocean itself as separate entities. We also falsely identify each wave as being distinct from all other waves. Real knowledge is gained and ignorance overcome when we see the bubble, the wave and the ocean as they really are – different facets of a single whole. Each wave is like the birth of an individual. Subsequent waves rise, and the previous waves subside; the two are related to each other. Or we can say that this process is like a seed and the tree. The seed is born from the tree, and the tree grows from the seed. The seed of one tree grows into another tree, and yet they remain related.

Categories of Individual

For the purposes of discussion we can group all individuals in three categories according to their traits and practices. First and foremost are those who come into the world with noble traits, are devoted to good deeds and are pure in their thoughts and actions. At the other end of the spectrum are those who drown in darkness and live in an unawakened state, with minds full of impurity. Purity is a manifestation of knowledge and impurity is a measure of ignorance. In the middle are those who are endowed with dynamism, no doubt, but are so propelled by strong desires that they often overlook or ignore the dividing line between the desirable and the beneficial.

If individuals arise from the same infinite ocean of supraphysical energy, how is it that some earn a place in the best category, some in the middle and some in the worst? This is because of the action-impact cycle, which shapes the inner core of an individual. Each one of our actions creates an impression on our mind, and each one of these impressions is like an imprint on a soft surface. Every such imprint encourages us to repeat that action, so that the imprint gets 'etched' more and more deeply in our mind as we repeat the action or class of actions. Some of these imprints travel from birth to birth, which explains why some people are born with one set of tendencies and some with another. These sets of tendencies constitute what is called our 'nature'.

We cannot speak of actions independently of the mind, because mind is the seat of all actions. Before an idea becomes an action, it arises in the mind as a seed of action. In this sense the mind is the 'body' in which action is wrapped. Action is the movement of energy in consciousness. All actions have their fruits or consequences and, similarly, every movement of energy inevitably bears its own fruit. When such an action comes to an end, the 'mind' in which that action has arisen also ceases, in a manner of speaking. When that mind ceases, no further action is possible.

Mind is perception; and perception is movement in consciousness. The expression of this movement is action, which is inevitably followed by the fruition of that specific action. Mind is an intention arising in the omnipotent and infinite consciousness, and is no different from infinite consciousness.[25] But our ordinary day-to-day 'mind' thinks otherwise; it clearly sees and believes in its own distinct identity.

Mind does not act, although we think that it does. Actions are performed by the organs of action, which are the hands, feet, eyes, nose and genitals. These organs are endowed with five sense capacities – touch, movement, sight, smell, procreation and excretion; and these sense capacities are inseparable from the mind. The organs of action strive to materialise whatever the mind thinks of, and so in that sense mind does manifest as action. The ultimate reality, however, is infinite consciousness, in which these concepts are conceived to exist. They arise spontaneously and, one could say, by sheer coincidence. When, out of ignorance, we identify ourselves as a separate individual, this is known as egotism. When we allow our mind to become lost and absorbed in countless thoughts as they come and go, this is known as individualised consciousness (jeeva).

It is often said that a person's life is shaped by his or her 'karma', and this is commonly thought to refer to a destiny which is unchangeable. Yet this is a superficial and somewhat erroneous view. Karma is action without an independent doer, especially when mind pursues the fruits of such action. It is pure movement in consciousness. When the mind entertains the notion 'I have seen this before' in relation to something seen or unseen, this is known as memory. And when the effects of past enjoyments and miseries remain in the field of consciousness, even though the effects themselves are unseen, this is known as a latent tendency. When our mind is entertained by sensations, this is known as the senses. When we become conscious of the truth that the division (overshadowing the underlying unity) is a product of ignorance, this is knowledge. When our mind moves in a false direction towards forgetfulness of the self and becomes deeply involved in projections and fantasies, this is known as impurity. When it remains unmanifest in the cosmic being, this is known as nature. When it creates confusion between reality and appearance, this is known as illusion. When it dissolves in the infinite, this is known as liberation. When it thinks 'I am bound', there is bondage; when it thinks 'I am free', there is freedom. In fact, when we enquire into the nature of the mind, all the created objects or appearances are seen to be simply its creations. Only infinite consciousness remains as that which is 'uncreated' by the mind.

The example of space is valuable to recall at this point, as a metaphor illustrating the interconnectedness of apparently distinct entities. Space is threefold: the infinite space of undivided consciousness, the finite space of divided consciousness, and the physical space in which the material worlds exist. The first of these, the infinite space of undivided consciousness, is that which exists in all individuals separately and collectively, inside and outside. It is witness to that which is real and to that which merely appears to be so. The second, the finite space of divided consciousness, is that which creates the divisions of time and pervades all beings. The third, the physical space, is that in which the other four gross material elements of air, water, fire and earth exist.

We must remember that in reality the divided finite space and physical space are not independent of the infinite space of undivided consciousness. This division of consciousness into three is simply an arbitrary invention, created to facilitate an understanding of this phenomenon. It is merely a suggestion aimed at enabling an individual to overcome ignorance. Those who are enlightened know that infinite consciousness is the only reality.

When that consciousness apparently thinks 'I am intelligent' or 'I am inert', that is the mind. When I think that 'I am intelligent' or 'I am bored' or 'I am sleepy', this is merely the deluded aspect of my consciousness at work. It is from this notion of 'I' that all the other imaginary physical and psychological factors evolve. At the level of ultimate reality, my consciousness is pure and free from the latent tendencies that are a consequence of the imprints laid down by my previous actions. Realising this is the attainment of self-knowledge.

To prepare the mind to recognise the delusion that wraps its perception is a huge challenge, for this delusion is so powerful that it resists even the light of wisdom shining upon it. Our ignorance and delusion have such a powerful hold on us that, under their spell, our mind even considers wisdom as its enemy. Our ignorance impels us to hurt ourself out of our own volition, and to make us run here and there in meaningless panic. Trapped in ignorance, we invite restlessness from our own latent desires.

And yet, the light of self-knowledge shines in every heart. When wisdom is gained, we realise that our uncontrolled mind is the source of our sorrow. Just recognising this truth causes ignorance to dissolve like the mist at sunrise. The change in our understanding becomes enduring as we persevere in gaining, nurturing and retaining the wisdom that comes from a spirit of enquiry.

To gain this understanding, the dialectics of the relationship between individualised consciousness and universal consciousness need to be internalised. We come to see that individualised consciousness is both different as well as not different from infinite consciousness, in much the same way as a wave is different and at the same time not different from the ocean.

MIND: APPARENT AND REAL

The energy of infinite consciousness pervades all things. It is the motion in air, the stability in earth, the void in space, and the power of self-consciousness ('I am') in created beings. It causes grief in the grief-stricken and elation in the joyous. The entire universe, including the 'I', is a manifestation of infinite consciousness; and the individualised consciousness is at the junction of infinite consciousness and matter.

The relationship between the body and the self is like that between the cloud and the wind, or the lotus and the bee. When the cloud is dispersed, the wind becomes one with space. When the lotus fades, the bee flies into the sky. The self (atma) is not destroyed when the body dies.[26]

From its 'home' of infinite consciousness, the mind displays its nature by spreading itself out to touch and magnify every little thing and make them all its own. In the twinkling of an eye it creates countless worlds, and in the twinkling of an eye it destroys them. Just as a versatile actor plays several roles one after the other, the mind assumes several aspects one after the other. It makes the unreal appear as real and vice versa.

In the beginning of creation, as bubbles arise in the infinite ocean, a division appears to occur in infinite consciousness, whereby the infinite appears to become both the observer and the observed. When the observer tries to comprehend or mentally 'grasp' the observed, confusion results from blending the real and the apparent. The concept of the finiteness of the self arises from this confusion.

The finite mind then generates within itself countless ideas which weaken and 'veil' it. As these become greatly magnified they leave their mark on the mind, forming the impressions of conditioning tendencies which we discussed earlier in this chapter. The 'veiled' mind sees a ghost where there is just a pillar. It pollutes all relationships; creating suspicion among friends, it makes enemies of them. Under its spell a person behaves like a drunkard who sees the world revolving around him or her. Such a mind, laden with tendencies, is the cause of delusions and endless sorrow. Hence, if this mind is mastered, everything else is mastered, including the senses – for if 'the mind is elsewhere', the taste of food that is being eaten is not really experienced; and we do not see what is right in front of us.

Mind flows with intensity towards its chosen object, seeking the fulfilment of its cravings. The cause of this movement in a particular direction is not obvious; like ripples on the surface of the ocean, such intense movement appears now here and now there, coming into being and then dying. Just as coolness is inseparable from ice, similarly this restless movement is inseparable from mind; for restlessness is the very nature of mind and is itself a form of ignorance. It is the seat of tendencies and of predispositions or conditioning.

Mind constantly swings like a pendulum between reality and appearance, between consciousness and inertness. It takes the very form of that which is being contemplated, whether this is natural or cultivated. When mind contemplates inert objects for some considerable time, it assumes a characteristic inertness. When the same mind is devoted to enquiry and wisdom, it shakes off all conditioning and returns to its original nature as pure consciousness.

This mental conditioning is not a manifestation of intelligence. However, as it is based on intelligence it has the appearance of intelligence. Although it is ever-changing, it creates the illusion of durability. And because of its proximity to infinite consciousness, it seems to be active. When infinite consciousness is realised, all of the conditioning comes to an end. At the heart of this realisation is the fact that mental conditioning has but a momentary existence. It is actually powerless, even while it seems to be very active – just as a mirror actively reflects the light of a lamp. Since it flows continuously, it seems to be permanent like a river – yet the water in a river at any particular point changes from moment to moment.

Mental conditioning seems to be real because it is able to veil reality; yet when we investigate it we discover that it is nothing. It seems to acquire strength and firmness in the same way as a flimsy fibre acquires great strength when rolled into a rope. This conditioning seems to grow, but in fact it does not – for as soon as we attempt to grasp it, it vanishes like the tip of a flame. It exists in the same way as things in a dream exist, and it creates confusion in the same way as people sitting in a moving boat see the shore moving. This ignorance or mental conditioning can only be mastered by becoming aware of its unreality.

Every object, entity or person in the cosmos – down to a blade of grass – is nothing but the self in which a 'veil' floats, creating a polarisation between an apparent subject and object. This veil is an idea, intention or thought existing in infinite consciousness, from which mind is born. And with the help of an idea or thought – that is, by bringing to an end the idea or thought that created it – it vanishes. As soon as we turn on the light, the darkness disappears. Similarly, ignorance disappears when we turn towards the light of the self. The seemingly endless stream of confusion generated by ignorance lasts only as long as a natural yearning for self-knowledge does not arise.

A mind that continually dwells on deluded or foolish ideas becomes ever more deluded. The same mind becomes enlightened when it continually dwells on enlightened and magnanimous ideas. Just as ignorance becomes firmly established through continuously nurturing deluded thoughts in the mind, so also does it dissolve through the gaining of self-knowledge and self-realisation. Those who calmly and continuously strive to be conscious of the self enjoy the fruits of their efforts by banishing ignorance forever and resting in a state of inner peace and tranquillity.

NOTES

1. Readers are particularly encouraged to marry their study of this section's contents with a reading of 'Section 5: Intelligence' in *The Ultimate Dialogue: The Fusion of Knowledge, Intelligence and Action*, 2007, pp.169 – 224, wherein RK Mishra examines in detail the nature of consciousness, the role of the intellect, and the functioning of the mind.
2. *Shiva Sutras, The Supreme Awakening*, 2002, revealed by Swami Lakshman Joo, p.75.
3. *ibid*, p.156.
4. John Hughes, 1997, *Self Realization in Kashmir Shaivism* ('The Oral Teachings of Swami Lakshman Joo'), p.22.
5. Mark SG Dyczkowski, 1987, *The Doctrine of Vibration*, New York: State University of New York Press, p.36.
6. *ibid* p.42.
7. See Appendix 1 for a list of the thirty-six tattwas that comprise the fabric of wholeness according to Kashmiri Shaivism.
8. Mark SG Dyczkowski, 1987, *The Doctrine of Vibration*, p.42.
9. ibid p.42.
10. *ibid* p.54.
11. *ibid* p.43.
12. *ibid* p.44.
13. *ibid* p.45.
14. *ibid* p.50.
15. *ibid* p.50.
16. *ibid* p.24.
17. *ibid* p.60.
18. *ibid* p.26.
19. *ibid* p.63.
20. *ibid* p.64.
21. *ibid* p.65.
22. *ibid* p.20.
23. *ibid* p.8.
24. *ibid* p.35.
25. The author has drawn upon a new translation of *The Yoga Vashishta*, the well-known Vedanta treatise in Sanskrit, and wishes to acknowledge his gratitude to the translator, Swami Venkateshananda of the Divine Life Society, Rishikesh, Uttaranchal, Himalaya. This new work was published by Swami Jivanmuktananda, in 2003 (fourth edition).
26. For a detailed study, see the chapter 'What Happens to Atma After Death?' in *The Cosmic Matrix* by the author, 2001.

SECTION FIVE

~

THE BUDDHIST PERSPECTIVE

Shakyamuni Buddha realised that nothing actually exists or 'stands apart' from all other things. What is most fundamental to existence is relationality, the interdependence of cause and effect.

Chapter 11

INTRODUCTION

1. BY WAY OF A DISCLAIMER

The author's engagement with Buddhism, in an intensive and deeper sense, followed from a desire to explore Shakyamuni Buddha's views on the concept of wholeness. In that process, the author began his encounter with the teachings of the thirteenth century Japanese monk Nichiren Daishonin (1222–1282), known as 'Nichiren Buddhism'. This tradition of Buddhism is founded on the belief that all living beings have the potential to achieve enlightenment – an idea that is the epitome of Mahayana Buddhism, one of the two principal divisions of Buddhism which arose in India after the passing of Shakyamuni Buddha.

Before we focus in more detail on Nichiren Buddhism, it should be noted that Buddhism is the most ancient 'religion' in the world. It is not a theistic tradition, and as such does not advocate a pattern of belief in a supreme deity or deities. There are no globally fixed Buddhist institutions or centralised authorities.

Western scholars often include 'Hinduism' among the world's major ancient religions. Yet in the author's view, the term 'Hinduism' is a convenience evolved by the Turkish and European schools to fit the numerous streams of Sanatana Dharma[1] into the western construction of a 'religion'. In actual fact, Sanatana Dharma is a way of life based on certain eternal (sanatana) principles, which include ethics, duties, responsibilities, relationships, and a comprehensive world view derived from the evolution of the cosmos and its integral relationship with human existence.

Buddhism stands at the intersection of Sanatana Dharma and the rise of the concept and practice of religion. This is why one comes across the essentials of Sanatana Dharma in Buddhism while at the same time encountering the flavour of 'religion' in the sense of the Abrahamic faiths – such as Judaism, Christianity and Islam – which are full-fledged 'religions'.

Buddhism as a whole has numerous schools, and even within Nichiren Daishonin's Buddhism there are many schools and sub-schools. The author of this work has relied upon the interpretation of Nichiren Buddhism by Daisaku Ikeda, the current President of Soka Gakkai International (SGI). (Readers will be introduced to Nichiren Buddhism and SGI later in this chapter.)

Against this brief introductory background, the author wishes to add the disclaimer that the views expressed herein, in no way show the writer's disrespect for various other schools of Buddhism nor for the various sub-schools of Nichiren Buddhism.

2. THE EVOLUTION OF BUDDHISM

Buddhism arose around 500 BC in response to the sufferings that characterise the human condition, and over time generated teachings which offer truly sustainable resolutions to the troubles and sufferings that afflict all sentient beings.

Originally promulgated by Siddhartha Gautama (563–483 BC most likely), who became known as the Buddha or 'Enlightened One', the teachings of Buddhism spread over the next half-millennium throughout southern, central, eastern and southeastern Asia. Buddhism's emphasis on the need for context-specific responses and resolutions tailored to each new linguistic and cultural environment resulted in a distinctive pattern through which it steadily diversified.

Buddhism's commitment to developing insight into the patterns of causal relationships has attracted considerable attention in the West, where it is seen to share common ground with modern science and technology – particularly as these have developed in the West. It is felt that Buddhism is well positioned to complement and also critically evaluate science and technology as knowledge-centred and practical enterprises.

Traditionally, Buddhist teachings and practices have been classified into three broad evolutionary streams: firstly, there is the *Hinayana* stream (literally 'Lesser Vehicle' but also known as the 'Small Vehicle', 'Basic Vehicle' or 'Foundation Vehicle'). The Hinayana stream is prevalent today in southeastern Asia; one prominent stream of Hinayana is referred to as the *Theravada* ('Way of the Elders'). Secondly, there is the *Mahayana* stream ('Great Vehicle'), which is most prevalent in eastern Asia; and thirdly the *Vajrayana* stream

('Diamond Vehicle'), which is associated primarily with Tibet and the societies and cultures of north-central Asia.

Scholars tend to divide the present-day adherents of Buddhism into three traditions as per the geographical / cultural areas: Hinayana/Theravada, East Asian Buddhism and Tibetan Buddhism. Some scholars prefer the two divisions of Theravada and Mahayana; in this classification, Mahayana includes both East Asian and Tibetan Buddhism. Buddhists themselves have a variety of other categories.

A comparative classification of the Buddha's teachings of the three periods arranges them in three categories according to the order of teaching and content, although the definition of these categories differs among the Buddhist schools. The *Agama Sutras* were taught in the first period – including the seminal Four Noble Truths teaching, given in order to refute attachment to the self or ego. In the Three Treatises school, the teaching of the first period corresponds to Hinayana while those of the second and third are divisions of Mahayana. They are: (1) the teaching that both mind and objective reality are real; (2) the teaching that objective reality is without substance and mind alone is real; and (3) the teaching that both mind and objective reality are without substance. The Three Treatises school defines the teaching of the third period as the complete teaching.

Mahayana, the 'Great Vehicle' set of teachings, is characterised by a spirit of compassion and altruism and expounds the lasting happiness of all beings through their attainment of enlightenment. To this end, *bodhisattva*[2] practice is the supreme means for bringing about the enlightenment of both oneself and others. This is in contrast to Hinayana, where the goal is personal salvation or attaining the state of *arhat*.[3]

The term 'Hinayana', literally translatable as 'lesser vehicle', was originally a pejorative term used by Mahayana Buddhists, who regarded the practitioners of these teachings as preoccupied solely with achieving personal emancipation and being indifferent to the salvation of others. The Hinayana teachings are represented by the doctrines of the Four Noble Truths, the Eightfold Noble Path, and the twelve-linked Chain of Causation. Hinayana practitioners regard earthly desires as the cause of suffering, and assert that suffering is eliminated only by eradicating them.

Critical insights and practical strategies have remained constant in the course of the historical development of Buddhism. These are expressed most succinctly in the Four Noble Truths teachings, in which Gautama Buddha taught that there is suffering; that suffering has a cause; that suffering has an end; and that there is a path that leads to the end of suffering. The fourth of the Noble Truths has come to be known as the Eightfold Noble Path, which in essence shows the way to overcome or dissolve one's negative patterns and resultant sufferings through the cultivation of complete and appropriate understanding, intentions, speech, action, livelihood, effort, mindfulness, and attentive virtuosity.

Rather than being a compromise position or a synthesis of a variety of contrasting views, the Buddhist viewpoint, known as the 'Middle Way', represents a return to that which is prior to the exclusion of the 'middle' between 'this' and 'that', between what 'is' and what 'is not'. This will be elaborated upon in the next chapter.

The teachings of the Buddha are aimed at the liberation of all sentient beings from suffering, and expound the principle that wisdom comes from understanding the three characteristics of existence: these are (a) that all conditioned phenomena are impermanent; (b) that all conditioned phenomena are not personal; and (c) that attachment to and desire for impermanent phenomena lead to suffering. 'Right Understanding' of the impermanent, non-self nature of phenomena, and of the fact that attachment to them causes suffering brings about 'Right Thought' – the aspiration or intention to be liberated from suffering and to understand the truth. The deepening of wisdom is enhanced when the lifestyle and mind are calmed through the practices of morality (*sheela*) and concentration (*samadhi*).

After a period of decline in the country of its origin, and stagnation elsewhere, Buddhism is now gaining new strength. The number of Buddhists in the world is estimated to be between 310 and 350 million. These estimates are uncertain because of complexities in the definition of who 'counts' as a Buddhist, as well as the situation prevailing in several countries, most notably China, Vietnam and North Korea. Theravada Buddhism, using Pāli as its scriptural language, is the dominant form of Buddhism in Cambodia, Laos, Thailand, Sri Lanka and Myanmar. East Asian forms of Mahayana Buddhism use scriptures in Chinese and are dominant in most of China, Japan, Korea, Taiwan, Singapore and Vietnam, as well as in the Chinese and Japanese communities within Indochina, Southeast Asia and the West. Tibetan Buddhism uses the Tibetan language and is found in Tibet and surrounding areas in India, Bhutan, Mongolia, Nepal and the Russian Federation.

3. NICHIREN BUDDHISM IN CONTEXT

Once Mahayana Buddhism had been introduced into China, this tradition gradually gave rise to various schools. One of the most important of these was founded by Chih-I (538-597) – also referred to as the Great Teacher T'ien-t'ai – and is known as the T'ien-t'ai school. It teaches that the *Lotus Sutra* is the highest of all the Mahayana sutras and that all things, both animate and inanimate, possess a dormant potential for enlightenment. This doctrine is summarised in the theory known as 'three thousand realms in a single moment of life'. The doctrines of the school were further clarified by Mio-lo (711-782), the sixth patriarch of the school.

T'ien-t'ai Buddhism was introduced to Japan as Tendai Buddhism in the early ninth century by the Great Teacher Dengyo, a Japanese priest who had gained a profound understanding of its doctrines in China. Later, in the thirteenth century, when Nichiren Daishonin studied in Japan, he reaffirmed his conviction that the *Lotus Sutra* constitutes the heart of Buddhism. According to his teachings, the workings of the universe are all subject to a single principle or law. By understanding that law, one can unlock the hidden potential in one's life and achieve perfect harmony with one's environment.

Nichiren Daishonin defined the universal law as Nam-Myōhō-Renge-Kyō, a formula that represents the essence of the *Lotus Sutra* and is known as the *daimoku*. Furthermore, he gave it concrete form by inscribing it upon the mandala known as the *Gohonzon* so that people could manifest their innate buddha wisdom and attain enlightenment. In his treatise titled *The Object of Devotion for*

Observing the Mind, he declares that chanting Nam-Myōhō-Renge-Kyō with faith in the Gohonzon, the crystallisation of the universal law, reveals one's buddha nature.

Various forms of Nichiren Buddhism have had great influence among certain sections of Japanese society at different times in the country's history. This Buddhist tradition is generally noted for its focus on the *Lotus Sutra* and an attendant belief that all beings have innate buddha nature and are therefore inherently capable of attaining enlightenment in their current form and present lifetime. It is also noted for locating itself in opposition to other forms of Japanese Buddhism – in particular the Zen, Pure Land, esoteric Shingon and Ritsu schools – which Nichiren considered to deviate from the orthodoxy of Mahayana Buddhism. Nichiren Buddhists believe that the spread of Nichiren's teachings and their effect on practitioners' lives will eventually bring about a peaceful, just and prosperous society.

Most Nichiren Buddhists believe that personal enlightenment can be achieved in this world within the practitioner's current lifetime, and their main practice is to chant the daimoku, the repeated recitation of the mantra (phrase) Nam-Myōhō-Renge-Kyō contained in the *Lotus Sutra*. Most Nichiren schools also recite the *Lotus Sutra* (in Japanese pronunciation of the Chinese text) to varying degrees in their respective versions daily or twice daily. Some recite the whole *Lotus Sutra*, while others recite only certain chapters, parts of chapters, or verses. Some chant it in front of Buddhist statues or images and the Gohonzon; others chant in front of statues or images of various types; yet others venerate only a particular Gohonzon and transcriptions of it. The Gohonzon is 'a scroll inscribed with many Chinese and two Sanskrit characters'.[4] A phrase Nichiren Daishonin uses to describe the Gohonzon is *Kanjin no honzon*, meaning the 'object of worship for observing one's mind (or life)'.[5] 'Just as a mirror can show us what we look like physically, so the Ghonzon is a mirror which enables us to "see" our lives in terms of the ten worlds.'[6]

According to Nichiren Daishonin, Shakyamuni Buddha expounded the *Lotus Sutra* in order to transmit the truth he had realised. The *Lotus Sutra* teaches that although all phenomena in the universe are impermanent, the ultimate reality permeating everything is eternally constant. Furthermore, this absolute or ultimate reality is not separated from individual phenomena but manifests itself in phenomena. We shall be exploring this further in a subsequent chapter in this section.

The mantra Nam-Myōhō-Renge-Kyō is the expression of the ultimate truth of life. *Namu* or *nam* derives from the Sanskrit word *namas* and means devotion, or the perfect fusion of one's own life with the eternal truth. The significance of namu is twofold: one meaning is to dedicate one's life to, or to fuse one's life with, the eternal unchanging truth. The other is that, through this fusion of one's life with the ultimate truth, one simultaneously draws forth infinite energy as well as inexhaustible wisdom which functions in accordance with the changing circumstances.

Myōhō-Renge-Kyō is also the title of the *Lotus Sutra* as it was translated into Chinese. Myōhō literally means the Mystic Law. *Myō* (mystic) signifies 'unfathomable', and *hō* means 'law'. This Law exists within the incomprehensible realm of life, beyond the reaches of the conceptual mind. In another interpretation, myō indicates the entity of the eternal truth and hō means all of the phenomena manifested by myō.

All things at one time or another assume the aspect of temporary existence which constantly changes, and at other times are in the state of non-substantiality (*ku*). No matter how the fundamental entity may manifest, in itself it is persistent and eternal. Phenomena (hō) are changeable but pervaded by a constant reality, which is myō.

Renge means 'lotus flower'. The lotus blooms and seeds itself at the same time and thus, represents the simultaneity of cause and effect, which is one expression of the Mystic Law. Simultaneous cause and effect means that essentially our future can be determined by present causes. Thus the law of cause and effect is also the principle of personal responsibility for one's own destiny. However, because the innermost depths of our lives are independent of the karma accumulated by our past deeds, we have the potential to create true happiness irrespective of karma. This is represented by the lotus, which grows and blooms in a muddy pond and yet is free from any defilement. Similarly, the innermost nature of our life remains untainted despite any negative causes we may have accumulated. Renge, thus, means 'to reveal the most fundamental nature of the reality of life'.

Finally, *kyō* means 'sutra', the voice or teaching of a Buddha. In a broader sense, it includes the activities of all living beings and of all phenomena in the universe. The Chinese character for kyō originally meant a 'warp of cloth', symbolising the continuity of life throughout the past, present and future.

4. SOKA GAKKAI INTERNATIONAL

Soka Gakkai International (SGI) is a Buddhist association with more than 12 million members, for whom Buddhism is a practical philosophy of individual empowerment and inner transformation. The promotion of peace, culture and education is central to SGI's activities.

Soka Gakkai (literally, 'Society for the Creation of Value') began in 1930 as a study group of reformist educators. Its founder, Tsunesaburo Makiguchi (1871-1944), was an author and educator, inspired by Nichiren Buddhism and passionately dedicated to the reform of the Japanese educational system. His theory of value-creating education, which he published in book form in 1930, is centred on a belief in the unlimited potential of every individual, and regards education as the lifelong pursuit of self-awareness, wisdom and development. Makiguchi's emphasis on independent thinking over rote learning, and self-motivation over blind obedience, directly challenged the Japanese authorities of the time who saw the role of education as moulding docile subjects of the state.

The 1930s saw the rise of militaristic nationalism in Japan, culminating in its entry into World War II. During this period, the militarist government imposed the State Shinto ideology on the population as a means of glorifying its war of aggression, and cracked down on all forms of dissidence. The refusal of Makiguchi and his closest associate Josei Toda (1900-58) to compromise their beliefs and lend support to the regime led to their arrest and imprisonment in 1943 on charges of being 'thought criminals'.

Despite attempts to persuade him to abandon his principles, Makiguchi held fast to his convictions and died in prison in 1944. Josei Toda survived the ordeal; he was released from prison a few weeks before the war ended. Amid the confusion of postwar Japan, he set out to rebuild Soka Gakkai, expanding its mission from the field of education to the betterment of society as a whole. He promoted an active, socially engaged form of Buddhism as a means of self-empowerment. He saw this as the way for people to overcome the obstacles in their lives and tap into their inner hope, confidence, courage and wisdom. This message especially resonated among the disenfranchised members of Japanese society, and before Toda's death in 1958 there were approximately one million Soka Gakkai members in the country of its origin. In 1957, Toda issued a forceful statement, calling on the youth to work for the abolition of nuclear weapons. This became the cornerstone of Soka Gakkai's peace activities, which the current president, Daisaku Ikeda, has been carrying on vigorously since assuming the leadership of SGI after the death of Josei Toda.

Daisaku Ikeda also experienced the horrors of war as a youth, and became determined to dedicate his life to building peace. He was 32 years old when he became president of Soka Gakkai in 1960. Under his leadership, the organisation has continued to grow and broaden its focus.

In 1975, in response to the needs of an increasingly international membership, Soka Gakkai International (SGI) was founded. Today it is a worldwide network with 82 registered constituent organisations and members in 190 countries and territories, sharing a common vision of a better world. SGI's philosophy underpins a movement promoting peace, culture and education. At its heart lies – and has always lain – a conviction in the unbounded potential of each individual, and the right of all beings to lead happy, fulfilled lives.

Chapter 12

WHOLENESS AND INTERCONNECTEDNESS

Nichiren Buddhism weaves the concept of wholeness in an intricate but fascinating framework of Ten Worlds, the mutual possession of these ten worlds, Ten Factors and Three Thousand Realms. All these comprise an interconnected web. This interconnectedness reflects the inseparable relationship between the individual and the environment, and the ability of each human being to influence both. In this chapter, we study various dimensions of this interconnectedness.

The Ten Worlds comprise the following:

1. Hell
2. Hunger
3. Animality
4. Anger
5. Tranquillity
6. Rapture
7. Learning

8. Partial Enlightenment
9. Bodhisattva
10. Buddhahood

The *Soka Gakkai Dictionary of Buddhism* explains: 'These Ten Worlds were viewed originally as distinct physical locations, each with its own particular inhabitants. The Lotus Sutra, however, teaches that each of the Ten Worlds contains all ten within it, making it possible to interpret them as potential states of life inherent in each individual being.'[7] As such, they indicate ten potential states or conditions that a person can manifest or experience.

THE TEN STATES OF EXISTENCE

These ever-changing conditions or states of existence are influenced by the individual's personal karma, which signifies potentials in the inner, unconscious realm of life created through one's actions in the past or present that manifest themselves as various results in the present or future. Karma means an act, an action, a former act leading to a future result, or a result. Buddhism interprets karma in two ways: as indicating three categories of action – mental, verbal, and physical – and as indicating a dormant force thereby produced. That is to say, our thought, speech and behaviour, both good and bad, imprint themselves as a latent force or potential in our life. This latent force, or karma, when activated by an external stimulus, produces a corresponding good or bad effect – happiness or suffering. There are also neutral acts, which produce neither good nor bad results. 'According to this concept of karma, one's actions in the past have shaped one's present reality, and one's actions in the present will in turn influence one's future. This law of karmic causality operates in perpetuity, carrying over from one lifetime to the next and remaining with one in the latent state between death and rebirth.'[8]

These states exist right here and now, rather than being regions on a different dimension or plane to which we go at the end of the current lifespan. When our balance in this life is disturbed, for example, calmness and contentment inevitably plunge into the trouble-filled states of Hell, Hunger, Animality or Anger. As noted earlier, each of the ten states includes all of the others within it, and every individual has the potential to manifest all ten states. The highest state is reached when we have the wisdom to realise that life continues in perfect harmony with the rhythm of the universe, and exists from the infinite past to the eternal future.

The Ten Worlds are ways of describing the subjective experience of individuals. Any one of the Ten Worlds can affect all the others, and each world 'possesses' or 'contains' all the others, bestowing upon the others its own particular 'flavour'. For example, the Hunger of a person dominated by Tranquillity may appear as a longing for something but without any action taken to achieve it; whereas the Hunger of someone in the grip of Animality can be seen in, for example, a desperate, grasping desire. Similarly, the Tranquillity of someone dominated by Animality could well manifest in a shopper sitting contentedly on the bus home, highly satisfied with the bargain he or she has managed to grab before anyone else; while the Tranquillity of someone who lives in the state of Hell could be a complete resignation or apathy in the face of suffering.

In effect, the mutual possession of the Ten Worlds multiplies these ten basic states of being, making them more subtle and complex. Life at each moment is endowed with the Ten Worlds. At the same time, each of the Ten Worlds is endowed with all the others, so that an entity of life actually possesses one hundred worlds. The mutual possession of the Ten Worlds is also the theoretical basis for explaining the possibility of moving from one state to another, from moment to moment.[9]

The Ten Worlds may also be explained as follows:[10] The world of Hell (1) indicates a condition in which living itself is misery and suffering and in which, devoid of all freedom, one's anger and rage become a source of further self-destruction. (2) The world of Hunger is a condition governed by endless desire for such things as food, profit, pleasure, power, recognition or fame, in which one is never truly satisfied. (3) The world of Animality is a condition driven by instinct and lacking in reason, morality, or wisdom with which to control oneself. In this condition, one is ruled by the 'law of the jungle', standing in fear of the strong but despising and looking down upon those weaker than oneself. Foolishness characterises the world of animals. (4) The world of Animosity or Anger is so called because it is characterised by persistent, although not necessarily overt, aggressiveness. It is a condition dominated by ego, in which excessive pride prevents one from revealing one's true self or seeing others as they really are. Compelled by the need to be superior to others or to surpass them at any cost, one may feign politeness and even flatter others while inwardly despising them. The worlds of Hell, hungry spirits, animals and asuras[6] are collectively called the 'four evil paths'.

(5) In the world of human beings, also called the world of Tranquillity, one tries to control one's desires and impulses with reason and act in harmony with one's surroundings and other people, while also aspiring for a higher state of life. (6) The world of heavenly beings, also called the world of Rapture, is a condition of contentment and joy that beings feel when released from suffering or upon satisfaction of some desire. It is a temporary, dependent state of joy which changes with changing circumstances.

The six worlds from Hell through to the World of Tranquillity are known as 'the six paths'. Beings in the six paths, or those who tend toward these states of life, are largely controlled by the restrictions of their surroundings and are therefore extremely vulnerable to changing circumstances.

The remaining states, in which beings transcend the uncertainty of the six paths, are called the four noble worlds: (7) The World of Learning is a condition in which one awakens to the impermanence of all things and the instability of the six paths. In this state, one dedicates oneself to creating a better life through self-reformation and self-development by learning from the ideas, knowledge and the experience of one's predecessors and contemporaries. (8) The World of Partial Enlightenment is a condition in which one perceives the impermanence of all phenomena and strives to free oneself from the sufferings of the six paths by gaining realisation of lasting truth through one's own observations and effort. Beings in this world are known as beings of the 'two vehicles', who are given more to the pursuit of self-perfection than to altruism. They are also willing to look squarely at the reality of death and seek the eternal, in contrast to those in the World of Heaven, who are distracted from life's harsh realities by an abundance of worldly pleasures.

(9) The World of the Bodhisattvas is a state of compassion in which one thinks of and works for others' happiness before seeking to attain happiness for oneself. The term 'bodhisattva' – which consists of *bodhi* (enlightenment) and *sattva* (beings) – refers to someone who seeks enlightenment in order to be able to lead others to enlightenment. Bodhisattvas find the way to self-perfection in altruism, working for the enlightenment of others before their own. (10) The World of Buddhas, or Buddhahood, is a state of perfect and absolute freedom in which one realises the true aspect of all phenomena, and therefore, the true nature of life.[11]

Ten Factors

Ten factors reflect the unchanging aspects of life common to all changing phenomena. These are: appearance, nature, entity, power, influence, internal cause, relation, latent effect, manifest effect, and their consistency from beginning to end. While the Ten Worlds express the differences among phenomena, the Ten Factors describe the pattern of existence common to all phenomena, which the entity of life manifests at each moment. For example, both the state of Hell and the state of Buddhahood, different though they are, have the Ten Factors in common. These Ten Factors bring us to an understanding of the wholeness or interconnectedness of the entirety of existence.

In brief, (1) Appearance refers to the attributes of things discernible from the outside, such as colour, form, shape and behaviour; (2) Nature is the inherent disposition or quality of a thing or being, which cannot be discerned from outside and which is unchanging and irreplaceable. The nature of fire, for instance, is unchanging and cannot be replaced by that of water. (3) Entity is the essence of life, which permeates and integrates appearance and nature. These first three factors describe the reality of life itself.

The next six factors, from the fourth – power – through to the ninth – manifest effect – explain the functions and workings of life. (4) Power is life's potential energy. (5) Influence is the action or movement produced when life's inherent power is activated. (6) Internal cause is the cause latent in life that produces an effect of the same quality as itself – good, evil, or neutral. (7) External Cause is the relationship of indirect causes to the internal cause – indirect causes being various conditions, both internal and external, that help the internal cause produce an effect. (8) Latent effect is the effect produced in life when an internal cause is activated through its relationship with various conditions. (9) Manifest effect is the tangible, perceivable result that emerges in time as an expression of a latent effect and therefore of an internal cause, again through its relationship with various conditions.

(10) Consistency from beginning to end is the unifying factor among the Ten Factors. It indicates that all of the other nine factors from the beginning (appearance) to the end (manifest effect) consistently and harmoniously express the same condition of existence at any given moment. This establishes the philosophical system of Three Thousand Realms in a single moment of life, of which the principle of the Ten Factors is a component.

T'IEN-T'AI'S THEORY OF 3000 LIFE-STATES IN EVERY MOMENT OF EXISTENCE

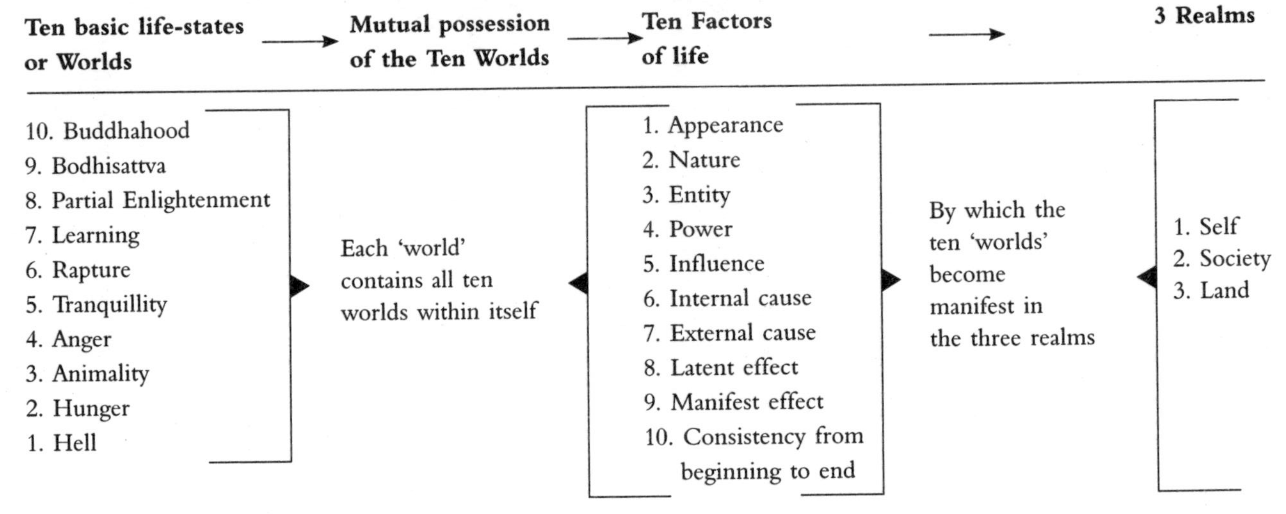

= 10 ⟶ 10 x 10 = 100 ⟶ 10 x 100 = 1000 ⟶ 1000 x 3 = 3000

Interconnectedness

Nichiren Buddhism explains that there is an ultimate 'realm' within our life called *amala*-consciousness or enlightenment, and that this place in our life is connected with the life of the universe.[12] It emphasises that 'life is at some level connected to everyone else in the world and… this relationship extends for generations backward and forward into the future. Maybe it is related to the "butterfly effect" physicists describe – that a seemingly random event in one part of the world often causes significant changes elsewhere.'[13]

In fact, 'enlightenment is an awakening to the true nature of life, including the profound realization of the interconnectedness of all things – the inseparable relationship between the individual and the environment and the ability of each human being to powerfully influence both. This realization leads individuals to assume personal responsibility for their own condition of life and the environment around them.'[14]

From the standpoint of the philosophy of the mutual possession of the Ten Worlds, Buddhahood should not be viewed as a state removed from the sufferings and imperfections of ordinary persons. Attaining Buddhahood does not mean becoming a special being. In this state, one still continues to work against and defeat the negative functions of life and transform any and all difficulties into causes for further development. It is a state of complete access to the boundless wisdom, compassion, courage and other qualities inherent in life; with these one can create harmony with and among others and between human life and nature.[15]

Chapter 13

INTERDEPENDENCE, SHUNYATA AND KARMA

As we noted in the previous chapter, the central belief and philosophy of Soka Gakkai – and indeed of other Buddhist traditions – is the potential and the right of all living beings to find happiness and overcome suffering. Different Buddhist schools teach a whole variety of methods for actualising the state of lasting happiness, free from suffering and the causes of suffering – a state known as 'enlightenment'.

Fundamental to all these techniques, methods of meditation and practical wisdom advice is the necessity of recognising and understanding the ultimate wholeness of all that exists. Terms such as 'relationality' or 'interdependence', 'impermanence', 'the natural law of cause and effect (karma)', and *shunyata* ('emptiness') are often used in combination to point to the truth of ultimate reality, the way things actually exist – as distinct from appearances, or the way we normally perceive things to exist.

Interdependence and Impermanence: Two Aspects of the One Truth

Let us consider these elements now. Interdependence is a key concept here – not simply as a theoretical appreciation of the inter-relationships we are often aware of in modern life but, more importantly, as an essential fact. We do not live in isolation. We live in harmony with our environment, of which we are an integral part. While each one of us is in a way unique – in that we shape an individual environment that is compatible with our own being – at the same time the formation of such an environment must coincide with the emergence of our life in this world. In other words, life extends its influence into the surroundings.

The advances in understanding made in the sciences of biology, bio-chemistry, physiology and quantum physics increasingly highlight the fact of interdependence. It is becoming more widely accepted in the modern world that all phenomena depend on other factors for their inception, sustainment and dissolution, and some scientists do concede that ultimately all phenomena in the universe exist as light and energy.

Concurrently with the physical sciences, the 'sciences of the mind' such as psychology, neurology and psychiatry have also been delving more deeply into the inter-connectedness of perception with appearance, thought with action, and mental health or lack of health with external and internal factors. However, all such physical or mental activities are simply functions which life expresses. They are not life itself, the true nature of which lies beyond the comprehension of these sciences.

Intrinsically connected to this fact of interdependence is the reality of impermanence. If it were not for change or impermanence, life would be untenable. Nothing would be able to function. Rivers would be unable to flow, seeds would not sprout, the sun would not rise in the firmament. The reality of change enables our hearts to beat, clocks to chime the hour, discoveries to be made, babies to be born.

Buddhism reminds us that there are several levels of change or impermanence, a fact of which we are commonly unaware. Most of us do take note of the gross forms of change in our environment, such as the leaves turning golden and falling from the trees in autumn, or the physical changes we see in our friends and relatives as they grow, develop and age. But beyond and behind all of these obvious forms of change or impermanence is the subtle, moment-by-moment changing nature of every atom, molecule and particle. Even something as seemingly immovable and unchanging as a mountain is in fact changing in every part of its great being with each moment. We may not live long enough to see it become a 'not-mountain' as its shape and being changes form over the longer period of time, but inevitably, such a change will occur.

THE TRUTH OF SHUNYATA

Buddhists are taught meditation practices which involve looking into their mind and observing the passing parade of thoughts and emotions, seeing how these arise in the mind, stay for a while and then dissolve. This constant flux and flow is testament to the truth of impermanence. Students are also asked to enquire of themselves in meditation: where do these thoughts come from? Where do they stay? And where do they go? When the dedicated student discovers that thoughts and emotions in fact have no root, no resting place and no destination, in that moment they glimpse the truth of shunyata. This term, commonly translated as 'emptiness', is the essence of reality and of experience. For, as it states in the *Heart Sutra*: 'Form is emptiness; emptiness also is form. Emptiness is no other than form; form is no other than emptiness.'[16]

These phrases point to the truth that all forms are comprised of constituent elements which, when they unite, give rise to phenomena; and when they separate, the result is dissolution of that particular form. Upon analysis, these constituent elements themselves prove to have no fixed or absolute existence. In other words, all phenomena are formed from elements which are ultimately non-substantial in nature, through a process of bonding which is also non-substantial. They are, therefore, transient phenomena in a state of constant flux.

The form and essence of each individual or being are integral and intertwined. The essence is not separate from the being, nor is it merely a product of the human imagination. Generally, a being can be defined as a manifestation of essence, which invariably takes on a form or physical aspect. Thus, the being contains both form as well as essence. These three – essence, form and being – exist as a united whole.

It is therefore a fact that 'Although the material and the spiritual are seen as two separate classes of phenomena, in essence they are indivisible.'[17] The ultimate reality of life expresses itself as the oneness of body and mind. 'According to Buddhism any attempt to try to understand the oneness of body and mind apart from the reality of life is to misunderstand it completely.'[18]

The most common English term given as a translation of the Sanskrit term 'shunyata' is 'emptiness'. This unfortunate interpretation misleadingly suggests a void or vacuum and thus, casts a nihilistic shadow over this explanation of reality. In fact, Buddhism charts a course between the two extremes of nihilism – that nothing really exists and therefore nothing has any real meaning – and eternalism – that phenomena have a real, independent, substantial existence from their own side. Buddhism upholds a view that is known as the 'Middle Way', expounding the truth that things both exist and do not exist. This is explained according to the two 'levels' or 'aspects' of relative truth and absolute (or ultimate) truth. Relative truth refers to the world of our normal perceptions, the world we see and move around in every day. Absolute truth refers to ultimate reality, the way things actually exist. What is important to realise is that these two aspects co-exist and are indivisible. We are only making a conceptual distinction between them here for the purposes of explanation.

On the relative level of our ordinary world, clearly things do have existence. We see and can touch the seemingly solid table in front of us; we go to school, graduate, get a job and pay our taxes. At the same time, however, according to the Buddhist teachings, none of this – including 'I' myself – exists of and by itself, independently of other factors. And none of it is permanent, as we noted earlier in the chapter. This is the absolute aspect of reality, the way things actually exist, which equates with a state of great openness known as shunyata.

Shunyata is 'empty' only in the sense that it is free from concepts or limitations. Its very essence is a vast, open, unbounded spaciousness. It is as open and vast as space itself, and yet it is not an entity. It is not some 'thing' to be realised. It is not a 'space' which the meditator creates in his or her own mind – since it has always been there, it cannot be created. It is described as being 'unborn and unceasing', 'beyond words, beyond thought, beyond description'. It is wholeness.

Its nature is a deep and limitless potential giving rise to everything. All phenomena – everything that exists – arise from this 'empty essence', as a wave manifests on the surface of the ocean. And, like the wave, phenomena too dissolve back into the 'empty essence' from which they have never been separate.

Lived experience of the natural law of cause and effect (karma) and an intellectual understanding of the truths of impermanence and interdependence which govern existence are signposts for the meditator on the path to realising the ultimate nature of reality. The truth of shunyata, when arrived at, is beyond concept and limitation and therefore cannot be realised by the ordinary mind. It can only be experienced by those who have readied their being for this revelation through consistent and dedicated meditative practice and reflection.

Sincere practitioners who realise shunyata understand the full import of these words by the twentieth century Zen master Shunryu Suzuki Roshi: 'What we call 'I' is just a swinging door which moves when we inhale and when we exhale. It just moves; that is all. When your mind is pure and calm enough to follow this movement, there is nothing: no 'I,' no world, no mind nor body, just a swinging door.'[19] Such a calm and pure mind is completely in touch and at home with the life-force.

Shakyamuni Buddha described all sentient beings as a collection of five changing processes: the physical body, feelings, perceptions, formations (or responses), and consciousness. A sense of self or 'I' arises from grasping at or identifying with these processes, which are actually always in a state of flux or flow. Recognising this facilitates insight into the reality of 'non-self' or egolessness, a notion which is central to all schools and traditions of Buddhism. Just as the term 'emptiness' is often misunderstood to mean a void or vacuum, the terms 'selflessness' or 'egolessness' are commonly misinterpreted as a kind of annihilation of the person or personality once the point of full understanding is reached. This is a false comprehension. Those who meet shunyata face-to-face, as it were, realise that while the self does exist in a relative or interdependent way (I can see my body, I can speak, I am recognised by others as the person I say I am, and so forth), in reality the self has no inherently independent existence from its own side. As stated earlier, just like all other phenomena, we are dependent upon causes and conditions in order to be born, to exist and to cease to exist.

At this point, a sceptic might declare: 'But what does it matter if things do or do not exist at the ultimate level? I'm here living my life and that is real enough for me.' This is where Buddhist practicality steps in, asserting that the wisdom which arises from understanding the true nature of the self and of all phenomena whittles away at the ego, which is the cause of all sufferings in the world. It is the ego which provokes greed, rage, competitiveness and lust, based on the false assumption that 'I' am a permanent solid entity responsible for getting what 'I' need and want and avoiding what 'I' don't want, in a dialectic of 'me' and 'them', 'mine' and 'yours'.

Egolessness, or shunyata, is the non-dual perspective that cuts through all this falsity and appreciates the futility of grasping at things that by their very nature are ungraspable, because they are only temporary. When we experience the vast openness of the life-force within, free of the shadows of the grasping ego-mind, we find within ourselves a deep well-spring of courage, humour, confidence, forgiveness and compassion.

In practical terms, Buddhists say, when we understand our interconnectedness with others – the wholeness of all phenomena – we can stop competing with them and live a life of kindness and ease. The fruit of this combination of wisdom and compassion is true, lasting happiness. All human activities aim at happiness; but real happiness should not be confused with the mere fulfilment of desires, which can offer only a temporary level of pleasure or happiness. The deeper and more lasting happiness depends neither on the object of desire or need, nor on our past accomplishments, nor on any other external factor. Its major 'ingredient' or component lies within us. Our happiness is directly related to the degree that we can draw upon our own life-force. In the process of working creatively with challenge and courage, as we attempt to understand and surmount our suffering we are led towards the state of absolute happiness. This is the way to develop vitality and wisdom.

The Natural Law of Karma

Even a glimpse of the wholeness and interconnectedness of all phenomena will lead us to appreciate that all our actions – physical, verbal and mental – have consequences, since we are an integral part of the whole. It is therefore incumbent upon us to remember and have respect for the natural law of karma or cause and effect, upon which human happiness is based. According to the Buddhist teachings, this relates principally to our inner life.

The Nichiren Buddhist teachings place karma in the context of nine levels of consciousness. The first five correspond to the five senses of sight, hearing, smell, taste and touch. The sixth consciousness integrates the perception of the five senses into coherent images and makes judgements about the external world. The seventh consciousness comprises the power of thinking, reflection and self-cognition.

The eighth level of consciousness, known as the *alaya*-consciousness, is the repository of all the experiences of the present and previous lifetimes – in a sense, this is the 'storehouse' of our karma. All the experiences of our life which take place through the first seven consciousnesses are accumulated as karma in this eighth consciousness, which at the same time exerts an influence on the workings of the seventh consciousness.

The ninth consciousness, called amala-consciousness, is the basis of all spiritual functions. Amala means 'pure' or 'undefiled'. Whereas the alaya-consciousness contains karmic impurities, the amala-consciousness lies within the innermost depths of life and remains pure, free from all the defilements of previous existences. It is the fundamental buddha nature, extending from the infinite past to the infinite future. It is ultimate reality.

Karma underpins the eternal flow of life. It is often misunderstood as a doctrine of fatalism or determinism, which virtually denies the existence of a free will. However,

Buddhism does not regard karma in this light, but rather reveals that we possess an inherent power with which to challenge 'fate' and break its chains. The causes we formed in the past bring about corresponding effects in the present, and our actions in the present in turn shape our future. It is possible to change our destiny and our future through establishing a deep connection with our innermost being, our life-force, and gaining an experiential understanding of the true nature of reality. As our understanding grows and deepens, our actions begin to change for the better, becoming increasingly aligned with a wholesome and compassionate wisdom.

A crucial factor in moving towards this inner transformation is our will-power. This operates at the conscious level of the human psyche, while karma exists at the unconscious level, or even deeper. We can effect a change in our destiny if our determination is strong enough. In fact, it is possible to emancipate ourselves totally from our negative karma. The awareness of our inherent, inexhaustible life-force generates the confidence to achieve this goal.

Such an inner transformation is the most fundamental of all transformations. Buddhist individuals have the power and capacity to bring about this inner revolution, if they engage themselves in persistent and dedicated spiritual effort. Any changes that occur in their everyday life result from the power gained through such self-transformation. This power is essentially the power of wisdom.

Gaining Ultimate Freedom

Buddhism teaches that the intertwined truths of interdependence, impermanence, karma and shunyata, when understood properly, are a cause of freedom for the individual. Any and every situation can be transformed to be of benefit because of the reality of shunyata, interdependence and impermanence. So rather than being cast down or depressed by the inevitability of change and dissolution, we experience true freedom and joy when we learn to let go of our compulsive clutching at things and experiences as if they were real, only to have them turn to dust in our hands. True freedom comes from realising that our thoughts and emotions are merely shadows that pass across the surface of the mind as clouds pass across the sky, leaving no trace when they have gone. The deepest part of ourself is pure, and always remains so.

As Buddhism makes no clear distinction between divinity and humanity, its teachings indicate the ability of all beings to attain enlightenment, just as Shakyamuni Buddha did. This is possible because of the fundamental buddha nature which exists within all beings. Even when this buddha nature is temporarily obscured by delusions, confusions, doubts and mental distractions, its essence is unchanging – and unchangeable. Once it is discovered within, its purity and unlimited potential are available to us.

It is this pure essence and freedom that Buddhism teaches its students to investigate, discover for themselves and then celebrate in the light of bliss and understanding.

NOTES

1. For further elaboration, see *Before the Beginning and After the End* by the author, 2000.
2. An enlightened being who, out of compassion, forgoes personal nirvana in order to bring others to liberation.
3. One who has attained enlightenment.
4. Richard Causton, 1995, *The Buddha in Daily Life: An Introduction to the Buddhism of Nichiren Daishonin*, p.13.
5. *ibid* p.231.
6. *ibid* p.231.
7. Soka Gakkai, 2002, *The Soka Gakkai Dictionary of Buddhism*, p.686.
8. *ibid* p.331.
9. Richard Causton, *op cit*, p.79.
10. Soka Gakkai, *op cit*, p.686.
11. Excerpted from the chapter, 'The Object of Devotion for Observing the Mind and States' of *The Writings of Nichiren Daishonin*, 1999, p.358.
12. Michael Lisagor, 2005, *Romancing the Buddha*, p.6.
13. *ibid* p.7.
14. *ibid* p.144.
15. *ibid* p.358.
16. from *The Sutra of the Heart of Transcendent Knowledge*, translated into English by the Nalanda Translation Committee.
17. *Fundamentals of Buddhism*, 1977, p.64.
18. *ibid* p.66.
19. Shunryu Suzuki Roshi, 1980, *Zen Mind, Beginners Mind,* p.29.

SECTION SIX

~

WHOLENESS IN THE 'MODERN' WORLD

Chapter 14

INTRODUCTION

In this section, we shall be looking briefly at the most popular, or widely accepted, approach of 'modern' scientists towards the universe, and we shall also investigate a few examples of courageous individuals who have posited a view of wholeness that contrasts with the common understanding of the same.

Particularly since the sixteenth century, what we may call 'modern' science has propagated the view that the universe is like a machine. In order to understand the universe, therefore, a perceived need is to 'break down' this machine into its component parts and then analyse each part individually. This approach, whatever its merits, has contributed significantly to the fragmentation of the human mind. In the grip of this widely accepted 'scientific' method, human beings have tended to forget that reality is not a sum of parts but, rather, an integral whole.

This 'modern' scientific methodology has had serious repercussions for the way knowledge has been pursued, organised and handed down from one generation to another; as a consequence, science today faces a serious crisis in its endeavour to comprehend reality. While the Cartesian order has been appropriate in analysing the world into separately existent parts (for example, particles or field elements), in both relativity theory and quantum theory the Cartesian order is leading to serious contradictions and confusions.

Art, science, technology and human work in general are today divided up into specialties, each considered to be separate in essence from the others. A sense of dissatisfaction with this approach led to initiatives being taken to set up interdisciplinary subjects, which were intended to unite these specialties. However, these have ultimately added further, separate fragments. Fragmentation is, in effect, an attempt to divide that which is really indivisible, and to try to 'untie' that which is not really 'untieable'.

For example, one school of thought in the world of physics asserts that light functions like waves, insofar as the energy of light glides through space in much the same way as ripples dance across the surface of a placid pond. Another school of thought maintains that light functions or behaves as particles in flight, rather like a stream of drops of water bursting out from a nozzle. Each of these points of view held dominance at one time or another, until in the first half of the twentieth century both theories were found to have validity.

Particle physicists discovered that subatomic particles cannot be considered to be made up of ultimate, simple building blocks which are separate and outside of each other. Increasingly, it is becoming clear that this analytical method is flawed. For example, in the bootstrap philosophy of Geoffrey Chew, the properties of any one particle are determined by all the other particles, so that every particle is a reflection of all the others. This structure – whereby a particle contains all other particles and is also contained in each of them – is fundamental, and will be explored in our chapter on the hologram and other examples later in this section. At this point, the author merely wishes to signal its significance as an indicator of the fundamental law of intrinsic wholeness, which is so often overlooked by contemporary scientists.

As mentioned at the beginning of this introductory chapter, not all scientists uphold the fragmentary view of nature, the universe and reality. Against the dominant perspective of the past 300 years, in which fragmentation prevailed over the holistic perspective in almost all branches of knowledge including medicine, education, physics, psychology and sociology, several scholars spoke out to warn against this lopsided view of engaging with reality.

These warning voices were either ignored, ridiculed or suppressed. In some cases, attempts were made to 'praise' them out of the domain of science by lauding them for their non-scientific pursuits rather than their scientific understandings. Goethe was one such example. He was a genius who had profound scientific insights; yet he was branded and celebrated more as a poet, novelist, playwright and natural philosopher. Of course, he *was* all these things, and much more. When his brilliance as a scientist refused to be clouded by such tributes, it was acknowledged – albeit with considerable reluctance – that he made important discoveries in connection with plant and animal life and evolved a non-Newtonian theory of character of light and colour.

Goethe is of particular interest in our current discussion because he strove so valiantly and persistently to locate the root of fragmentation. He noted that: 'Modern science can only approach the whole as if it were a thing among things. Thus the scientist tries to grasp the whole as an object for interrogation.' Therefore, science today, 'by virtue of the method, which is its hallmark, is left with a fragmented world of things which it must then try to put together.'[1] Recognising that the experience of authentic wholeness requires a new style of learning, Goethe regretted the fact that this was largely ignored in the schools and universities of his time. He underlined the fact that: 'Science believes itself to be objective, but is in essence subjective because the witness is compelled to answer questions which the scientist himself has formulated. Scientists never notice the circularity in this because they believe they hear the voice of nature speaking, not realizing that it is the transposed echo of their own voice.'[2]

He also made this salient point: 'Wholeness is very different from how we have become accustomed to thinking of it in modern science.' And he acknowledged: 'Modern physics is true but it does not mean that it is fundamental. It cannot be the foundation upon which everything else, human beings included, depends.' The fact that the foundations of science are cultural-historical 'does put a different perspective on the fundamentalist claims made on behalf of science by some of its self-appointed missionaries today.' In light of the new discoveries in the history and philosophy of science, he said, 'the claims (of modern science) to have found the ultimate basis of reality look like no more than quaint relics from a bygone age.'[3]

Viktor Schauberger is another case in point. A scientific observer of extraordinary perspicacity and brilliance of innovation, Schauberger understood that 'Nature is not served by rigid laws, but by rhythmical, reciprocal processes,'[4] and accordingly he developed technologies that sought to locate the relationship of human beings with nature in a mutually nourishing manner. Yet instead of being hailed for his amazing insights, he was harassed and persecuted in a heartless manner for his steadfast stance against humankind's rapacious exploitation of nature and the destructive application of technology.

Schauberger's aim was to try to perceive the dynamic reality behind what he saw as physical illusion. He gained a profound comprehension of the sublime energetic interdependencies upon which life at all its levels is founded. He claimed that, by and large, we human beings are extremely superficial, looking for and only seeing direct relations between cause and effect, whereas nature always moves indirectly. 'But worse than this, in our ignorance of the unseen dynamic behind the seen manifestation, we mistake the effect for the cause, greatly compounding this error by failing to see that an effect becomes the cause for a further effect in an endless chain of causes and effects.'[5]

He came to the conclusion – which he articulated candidly – that western science and education suffer from a myopic compartmentalisation of mind, and that 'today's science thinks too primitively; indeed it could be said that its thinking is an octave too low. For this reason it is principally to blame for the state of affairs we are experiencing today.'[6]

More recently, scientist David Bohm has been another powerful voice raised in support of a critical understanding of the wholeness of all of existence. In recognising the confusion brought about by a 'deep and radical fragmentation' that prevails in humankind's attempts to comprehend reality according to the laws of physicality, he notes that contemporary physicists have a tendency to avoid the issue by refuting the significance of over-arching views about the nature of reality, believing instead that it will suffice to examine the parts of the whole in isolation from each other. But, as Bohm points out, the word 'health' in the English language is based on an Anglo-Saxon world 'hale', which meant 'whole' – in other words, to be healthy is to be whole.

As we proceed with our study in this section of the work, we shall examine the theoretical and practical dimensions of fragmentation and wholeness in 'modern' science. With the assistance of Goethe, Bohm and Schauberger, we shall take our readers on an exciting journey towards a real understanding and appreciation of the underlying wholeness of our existence. In the process, we hope to aid a reversal of the fragmentation world view and thus contribute to other attempts being made to avert its dangerous consequences.

EDITOR'S NOTE:

The chapters on David Bohm's and Schauberger's work in this section are incomplete. It was RK Mishra's intention to explore thoroughly the key findings and insights of these notable men of science and vision and to present them here in this work. We include the beginnings of his research in this section, in the hope that our readers will be stimulated to pursue their study of wholeness through the writings of these courageous and original thinkers.

Chapter 15

WHOLENESS IN NATURE: GOETHE'S PERSPECTIVE

Science of nature has one goal,
To find both manyness and whole.[7]

If you want to reach the infinite,
Explore every aspect of the finite.[8]

The mainstream of mathematical physics from Newton onwards tended to see mankind and nature as entirely external to one another. The Goethean perspective replaced this external dualism with a deeper understanding of the relationship between nature and mankind, one in which they belong together.

This relationship of interconnectedness has the potential to lead to a technology in which nature and human beings co-operate to their mutual enhancement. While Francis Bacon advocated science as power over nature, Goethe's science made itself utterly identical with the object. Goethe took science beyond mathematical abstractions and microscopic explanations, towards the lived experience of phenomena.

In Goethe's view a phenomenon is only partly visible, and the task of science is to make it wholly visible. This can be achieved by exploring the inner dimensionality of the phenomenon being studied. According to Goethe, each phenomenon is a manifestation of the one, the concrete mode of unity. It is 'multiplicity within unity, instead of unity abstracted from multiplicity. This concrete mode of unity is one and many at the same time. It permits diversity within unity, whereas the abstract mode of unity excludes diversity and allows only uniformity.'[9]

Science, for Goethe, was a method of consciousness-raising. However, it could only function as such when brought into living connection with all human faculties. 'Goethe's refusal to abandon the sensory realm gave to his scientific endeavours a freshness and an accessibility contemporary science lacks. Goethe was pursuing a type of knowledge that enriches rather than impoverishes human experience of nature.'[10]

In contrast, western scientific culture is ready to defer to the pre-existent categories of the established sciences, and consequently has reached a situation in which there is no longer a mental openness towards phenomena. It has been said that the advances in specialised scientific knowledge have encouraged a chronic laziness with regard to the everyday observation of nature. This applies to non-scientists and to scientists alike.

The result is a grave crisis for humankind, which functions in a state of rupture from the natural world. As a result, the resensitisation of our day-to-day consciousness regarding nature has become an urgent task. Nature today, is in need of being healed, in direct proportion to the extent to which our consciousness of nature is sick. This is the key to restoring a harmonious relationship between human beings and the natural world; for the issue is not simply the degradation of nature, but the degradation of our awareness of nature.

In his essay 'On the History of the Physical Interpretation of Nature', Heisenberg writes of 'the basis of scientific progress since Newton's time as having involved a sacrifice of living and immediate understanding.' He accepts that 'this was the real reason that Goethe engaged in bitter struggle against Newton's physical optics.'[11] Heisenberg heard Goethe's voice virtually as the troubled conscience of the modern scientist.

Rather than advocating a path of manipulation and control, Goethe was a pioneer of a holistic and qualitative science of nature. 'As conceived by Goethe, science is as much an inner path of spiritual development as it is a discipline aimed at accumulating knowledge of the physical world. Rather than simply making new discoveries and propounding new theories on the basis of ever more refined techniques of physical observation, the aim of science is to open the eyes and mind of the beholder of nature to what is spiritually at work within, or at the root of, the observed physical phenomena.'[12] This involves 'not only a rigorous training of our faculties of observation and thinking, but also of other human faculties which can attune us to the spiritual dimension that underlies and interpenetrates the physical: faculties such as feeling, imagination and intuition.'[13]

Instruments of Analysis

The foundations of the modern scientific enterprise were laid in the sixteenth and seventeenth centuries. Since then it has been an almost unquestioned assumption within mainstream science that all experienced qualities and forms in nature are made accessible through various instruments and analytical techniques. It has also been assumed that 'phenomena, unlike those we meet in our normal experience, are susceptible to exact chemical and mathematical analysis.'[14]

For Goethe, human beings are the most powerful and exact instruments, if their sensibilities are sufficiently refined. This proposition contradicts what most contemporary scientists take for granted and runs counter to the way in which science has been practised in modern times, as noted above. For, it is argued, without the development of ever more sophisticated non-human instruments, most of the advances in modern scientific knowledge would not have occurred. So it seems contrary to common sense to claim that the human being is the most exact instrument, when there are instruments far more sensitive than any human being. Goethe did not, in fact, rule out the benefits of ever more precise observation through the use of instruments. He acknowledged their value, but maintained that 'unless these observations were brought back into connection with the lived human relationship to nature, they would inevitably lead to a one-sided and distorted understanding of the world.'[15]

For example: 'modern biology has come to view living organisms as little more than the epi-phenomenon of groups of genes – "the DNA replicators" – which have a microscopic existence inside them. As a consequence, the organism as a living whole disappeared from view. Today, this type of explanation has become so much a part of understanding nature that any other kind of explanation is generally regarded as unscientific.'[16]

Modern science has also given rise to endless profusion, fragmentation and complexity. This is not surprising. A crisis arises when a field of knowledge matures enough to become a 'science'. Those who focus on details and treat them as separate are set against those who have their eye on the universal and try to fit the particular into it. To escape this gridlock, we need to recover the element of simplicity.

The living development of organisms has an overall coherence, and an organisational principle is required to enable human minds to perceive it. This is not possible with the kind of minute analysis that characterises modern research in biology, for example. In observing objects of nature, especially those that are alive, scientists often think that the best way of gaining insight into the relationship between their inner nature and the effects they produce is to divide them into their constituent parts.

Of course, what is alive *can* be dissected into its component parts – but from these parts it will be impossible to restore it and bring it back to life. There is a need to 'understand living formation as such, to grasp their outward, visible, tangible parts in context, to see these parts as an indication of what lies within and thereby gain some understanding of the whole through an exercise of intuitive perception.'[17] For Goethe, science should attend to wholes as well as parts. It should be a fusion of directly experienced qualities, as much as indirectly experienced microscopic ones.

In modern physics, experiments are set apart, as it were, from the human being. Physics refuses to recognise anything in nature that is not shown by artificial instruments. It even uses this as a measure of its accomplishments. The same applies to calculation: modern science refuses to reckon with the fact that many things cannot be calculated, and that there are other things which defy experimentation. Conversely, Goethe believed that human beings are adequately equipped for all genuine needs on earth if they trust their senses and develop them. Experiencing, looking, observing, contemplating, connecting, discovering and inventing are mental activities which, singly and severally, are exercised a thousandfold by more or less gifted people. From these various powers and many other related ones, nature has excluded no one.[18]

'All of us experience, often unknowingly, the conveyance of manyness in oneness, as we wade through life. The professional musician hears, in an orchestral performance, every instrument and every single tone. On the other hand, one unacquainted with the art is wrapped in the massive effect of the whole. You can see in a green or flowery meadow only a pleasant view, while the eye of a botanist discovers endless detail of the most varied plants and grasses.'[19]

The 'modern' mind assumes that knowledge can be acquired by learning. But Goethe maintains that 'there are things which cannot be known only by learning. The son, from pure learning, does not know his own father. Similarly, in science we find people who can neither see nor hear, through sheer learning and hypothesis. Such people are so occupied by what is revolving in themselves that they are like someone in a passion, who passes their close friends in the street without seeing them.'[20]

If we are to understand nature fully, we need to explore many different types of knowing and avoid restricting ourselves to one single style of acquiring knowledge. The scientist sees one aspect of nature, the metaphysician another, the poet yet another. Within the sciences, too, a given phenomenon can be apprehended from a variety of different standpoints, and from within the range of different but complementary disciplines. Each mode of human observation is sensitive to just one dimension of nature's multi-dimensional existence. 'Nature has no system; she has – she is – life and development from an unknown centre toward an unknowable periphery.'[21] Thus, the observation of nature is limitless, whether we make distinctions among the least particles or pursue the whole by following the trail far and wide.

Goethe explains that the fundamental characteristics of any individual organism are 'to divide, to unite, to merge into the universal, to abide in the particular, to transform itself, to define itself, and, as living things tend to appear under a thousand conditions, to arise and vanish, to solidify and melt, to freeze and flow, to expand and contract. Since these effects occur together, any or all may occur at the same moment. Genesis and decay, creation and destruction, birth and death, joy and pain, all are interwoven with equal effect and weight; thus even the most isolated event always presents itself as an image and metaphor for the most universal.'[22]

These observations lead to the inevitable conclusion that whatever appears in the world must divide if it is to appear at all; and that which has been divided seeks itself again, can return to itself and reunite. Students of the Upanishads will hear in Goethe's explanation echoes of the concept that unity and multiplicity are one and the same (*ekoham bahusyami*). All natural phenomena possess either an original duality capable of being merged in unity, or an original unity capable of becoming a duality. Separating what is united and uniting what is separate is the life of nature.[23] This is the breathing in and out of the world in which we move and have our being. In organic nature, the whole is always prior to the parts of which it is composed. And while analytic work gives a clear perception of the parts, the ultimate goal of scientific endeavour should be to arrive at a perception of the underlying unity which binds the parts together. These two activities are as inseparable as inhaling and exhaling.

As Goethe says: 'Nothing happens in living nature that does not bear some relation to the whole. Every one thing exists for the sake of all things and all for the sake of one. Nature, despite her seeming diversity, is always a unity, a whole; and thus, when she manifests herself in any part of that whole, the rest must serve as a basis for that particular manifestation, and the latter must have a relationship to the rest of the system.'[24] If we are to truly understand reality, we must proceed in our exploration from the whole to the parts and from the parts to the whole. 'And the more vitally these two functions from the mind are conjoined, like breathing in and out, the better it will be for science and its friends.... If you would seek comfort in the whole, you must learn to discover the whole in the smallest part.'[25]

Quantifying Reality

For Goethe, mathematics is, no doubt, the most sublime and useful science, as long as it is applied judiciously and in its proper place. He refused to accept that things only exist when they can be mathematically demonstrated: 'It would be foolish for a man not to believe in his mistress' love because she could not prove it to him mathematically. She can mathematically prove her dowry, but not her love.'[26]

In short, Goethe believed that mathematics cannot give us a complete account of reality as its province is restricted to the measurable, whereas the qualitative aspect of nature is not susceptible to measurement. Quantity and quality must be viewed as two poles of material existence. 'A science of nature based on mathematical methods alone will result in a particular view of nature that would need to be complemented by a qualitative science.' Moreover, he maintains that 'the qualitative aspect of nature has primacy over the quantitative. This is because the qualitative is what is given to our immediate experience.'[27] In other words, as human beings in relationship with our world, our actual experience is of qualities rather than of numbers or mathematical formulae.

Goethe knew that the act of scientific discovery is a perception of meaning, requiring interpretation by the mental faculties of impressions received through the sensory faculties of the scientist. For example: 'The discovery that there are mountains on the moon was a perception of meaning, and not the purely sensory experience it is represented as being.'[28] Therefore, it can be said that the essence of a discovery lies in the non-empirical factor of cognition.

Once cognition has occurred, the mind swiftly organises the experience, in the process of which a temporal framework is imposed whereby the experience becomes 'organised' into a linear sequence of moments. 'We impose this framework intellectually on nature, with the results that we imagine nature as being organized in a liner, temporal sequence, whereupon it becomes possible to describe motion and change quantitatively.'[29]

Goethe's scientific methodology was quite different. It was based on the assumption that the human mind has the capacity to enter into the essence of phenomena and to lay hold of principles which, once grasped, alter one's perception of, and relationship to, these phenomena. The Goethean scientist seeks to participate in the objects investigated to such a degree that the mind makes itself one with the object, thereby overcoming the sense of separateness which characterises our normal experience of ourselves in relation to the world.

'Nature, however manifold it may appear, is nevertheless always a single entity, a unity; and thus, whenever it manifests itself in part, all the rest must serve as a fountain for the part, and the part must be related to all the rest. To grasp that the sky is blue everywhere, one does not have to travel around the world.'[30]

The concepts of being and totality are one and the same. 'When pursuing the concept as far as possible, we say that we are conceiving of the infinite. But we cannot think of the infinite, or of total existence. We can conceive only of things which are finite or made finite by our mind, that is, the infinite is conceivable only in so far as we can imagine total existence – but this task lies beyond the power of the finite mind.'[31]

Although all finite beings exist within the infinite, they are not parts of the infinite; instead, they *partake of* the infinite. The things we call the parts in every living being are so inseparable from the whole that they may be understood only in and with the whole.

Nature has neither core
Nor outer ring,
Being all things at once.
It's yourself you should scrutinise to see
Whether you're centre or periphery.[32]

Chapter 16

THE HOLOGRAM AND OTHER EXAMPLES[33]

In his remarkable work on Goethe's way of science, Henri Bortoft has focused extensively on several examples which explain the concept of the wholeness of nature. These include the hologram, the night sky, and the natural life of plants. In this chapter, we reprint extracts of his discourse in order to reflect upon their meaning and implications for our study.

The Hologram

While the ordinary photographic plate records reproduce a flat image of an illuminated object, the hologram does not record an image of the object photographed. Instead it provides an *optical reconstruction* of the original object. When the hologram plate itself is illuminated by the coherent light from the laser with which it was produced, the optical effect is exactly as if the original object were being observed.

Bortoft explains that 'a hologram has several remarkable properties in addition to those related to the three-dimensional nature of the optical reconstruction which it permits. The particular property which is of direct concern in understanding wholeness is the pervasiveness of the whole optical object throughout the plate. If the hologram plate is broken into fragments and one fragment is illuminated, it is found that the same three-dimensional optical reconstruction of the original object is produced.'[34]

The entire original object can be optically reconstructed from any fragment of the original hologram. In orthodox photography, the image fragments with the plate; whereas in holography, the image remains undivided when the plate is fragmented. The hologram example shows how the whole is present in the parts – the entire picture is wholly present in each part of the plate. Therefore, it would not be true in this case to say that the whole is made up of its parts.

The example of the hologram helps us to see that the essence of the whole is that it *is* whole. No matter how often we break the hologram plate, the picture is undivided. It remains whole even while becoming many. This essential irreducibility of the whole is so strong that it seems inconceivable for the whole to have parts.

This is quite the opposite of the commonly held view about the relation between parts and whole, which is to effectively deny the primacy of the whole. We are accustomed to thinking of going from parts to whole. We see the whole as developing through the integration of its parts. This approach places the whole in a secondary position to its parts, because it necessarily implies that the whole comes *after* the parts. In other words, a linear sequence is implicit here: first we look at the parts, then the whole.

The primacy of the whole, as seen in the hologram, should encourage us to reverse the direction of this way of thinking. It makes us realise that we cannot separate parts and whole into disjointed positions, for the whole imparts itself. It is accomplished through the parts it fulfils.

If the hologram plate were to be broken into fractions, the whole would not be broken. The whole is present in each fraction, although its presence diminishes as the fractioning proceeds. Starting from the opposite position, we could put many fractions together to build up the totality. As we do so, the whole world would emerge, and it would manifest more fully as we approach the totality. But in doing this we would not be building up the whole, for it is already present in the fractions. In reality, the whole emerges *simultaneously with* the accumulation of its parts, not because it is the sum of the parts but because it is immanent within them.

Inasmuch as the whole is whole, it is neither earlier nor later. To say that the whole is not later than the parts is not to say that we do not put parts together. Of course, we do – consider the action of writing, for example. But the fact that we often put parts together does not mean that in so doing we put the whole together. Similarly, to say that the whole is not earlier than the parts is not to deny the primacy of the whole. And, at the same time, to assert the primacy of the whole is not to maintain that it is dominant, in the sense of having an external superiority over the parts.

A part is only a part according to the emergence of the whole which it serves. The hazard of emergence is such that the whole depends on the parts to be able to come forth, and the parts depend on the coming forth of the whole to be significant instead of superficial. The recognition of a part is possible only through the coming to presence of the whole. Thus, we cannot separate part and whole into disjointed positions.

Our Night-time World

Bohm asserts that our experience of the night-time world is another instance in which wholeness becomes apparent when placed under scrutiny. Bortoft explains that we are only able to see our night-time world because light carries the stars to us. This means that the vast expanse of sky, in its entirety or wholeness, must be present in the light which passes through the small aperture of the pupil into the human eye. He notes that others looking at the same expanse of night sky, whether they are standing next to us or in different locations, also see the stars we see, and hence the stars seen in the heavens are all present in the light which is at anyone's eye-point. This indicates that the totality of the night sky is contained in each small region of space (such as the pupil of an eye). When we use optical instruments such as a telescope, we are simply reclaiming more of that light.

Bortoft muses: 'If we set off in imagination to find what it would be like to be light, we come to a condition in which here is everywhere and everywhere is here. The night sky is a space which is one whole, enfolded in an infinite number of points and yet including all within itself.'[35]

Looking at the Universe

Similarly, matter behaves in an unexpectedly holistic way at both the macroscopic and the microscopic level. We tend to think of the large-scale universe of matter as being made of separate and independent masses interacting with one another through the force of gravity. Yet the viewpoint which emerges from modern physics is very different from this traditional conception. It is now believed that mass is not an intrinsic property of a body. It is, in fact, a reflection of the whole of the rest of the universe in that body. So, instead of trying to understand the universe by extrapolating from the local environment here and now to the universe as a whole, it may be useful to reverse the relationship and understand the local environment as being the result of the rest of the universe.

Particle physicists have found that subatomic particles cannot be considered as ultimate, simple building blocks which are separate and outside of each other. Increasingly, it becomes clear that analysis in this traditional way is inappropriate at the microscopic level. Thus, in the bootstrap philosophy of Geoffrey Chew, the properties of any one particle are determined by all the other particles, so that every particle is a reflection of all the others. This structure, whereby a particle contains all other particles and is also contained in each of them, is expressed succinctly in the phrase: 'every particle consists of all other particles'.

Reading a Written Text

What happens when we read a written text? Successful reading is not just a matter of saying the words. It is an act of interpretation – but not interpretation in the subjective sense. True interpretation conveys the meaning of the text; it conveys the sense of what passes through or goes between.

We often say, 'I see', when we wish to indicate that we have grasped something. If we try to look at what we imagine is in our grasp, however, we find ourselves empty-handed. It does not take much experimentation here to realise that meaning cannot be grasped like an object.

The meaning of a text must have something to do with the whole text. What we come to here is the fundamental distinction between whole and totality. The meaning is the whole of the text, but this whole is not the same as the totality of the text. That there is a difference between the whole and totality is clearly demonstrated by the fact that we do not need the totality of the text in order to understand its meaning. We do not have the totality of the text when we read it, but only one bit after another. The meaning of the text is discerned and disclosed with progressive immanence throughout the reading of the text.

The meaning of the text can therefore be compared to the whole picture which can be reconstructed from the hologram plate. This is the sense in which the meaning of the text is the whole. The whole is not the totality, but the whole emerges most fully and completely through the totality. The whole is present throughout all of the text, so that it is present in any part of the text. It is the presence of the whole in any part of the text which constitutes the meaning of that part of the text. Indeed, we can sometimes find that just by understanding a single passage the whole meaning of the text becomes suddenly illuminated for us. Likewise, the meaning of a sentence has the unity of a whole. We reach the meaning of the sentence through the meaning of the words, yet the meaning of the words in that sentence is determined by the meaning of the sentence as a whole. (See the chapter, 'Sound and Communication' for a more detailed exploration of this topic.)

Everything we encounter in the world can be said to be either one thing or another, either this or that, either before or after, and so on. Wherever we look, there are different things to be distinguished from one another: this book here, that pen there, the table underneath, and so on. Each thing is outside the other, and all things are separate from one another.

We cannot know the whole in the same way that we know things, because we cannot recognise the whole as a thing. If the whole were available to be recognised in the same way as we recognise the things which surround us, then the whole would be counted as one of those things. We could point and say: 'Here is this, and there is that, and that is the whole over there.' If we had the power of such recognition, we would know the whole in the same way that we know its parts, for the whole itself would simply be numbered among its parts. The whole would be outside its parts in the same way that each part is outside all the other parts. But the whole comes into presence within its parts, and that is why we cannot encounter the whole in the same way that we encounter the parts.

We should not think of the whole as if it were a thing. Although our everyday awareness is occupied with things, the whole is absent from this awareness because it is not a thing among things. The whole is no-thing, and in comparison with the awareness of 'something', no-thing is 'nothing'.

We have an illustration immediately on hand with the experience of reading. We do not take the meaning of a sentence to be a word. The meaning of a sentence is no-word. But evidently this is not the same as nothing, for if it were we could never read. The whole becomes present within parts, but from the standpoint of the awareness which grasps the external parts, the whole is an absence. This absence, however, is not the same as nothing. Rather, it is an active absence. We do not try to be aware of the whole as if we could grasp it like a part, but instead let ourselves be open to be moved by the whole.

Enacting a Play

Another illustration of active absence is provided by the enacting of a play. Actors do not stand away from a part as if it were an object. By entering into a part, they enter into the play. If the play is constructed well, the whole play comes into presence within the parts, so that the actors encounter the play through their part. But they do not encounter the play as an object of knowledge over which they can stand, like the lines they learn. They encounter the play in their part as an active absence which can begin to move them. When this happens, they begin to be acted by the play, instead of trying to act the play. The actors no longer impose themselves on the play as if it were an object to be mastered, but listen to the play and allow themselves to be moved by it. They enter into their parts in such a way that the play speaks through them. While their awareness is occupied with the lines to be spoken, they encounter the whole which is the play – not as an object but as an active absence.

The Wholeness of the Animal Kingdom

In his zoological study, *Man and Mammals*,[36] Wolfgang Schad shows how all mammals can be understood in terms of the way in which the whole is present in the parts. In addition, he demonstrates how each mammal can be understood in terms of its own overall organisation. Every detail of an animal is a reflection of its basic organisation. Thus, he does not begin by replacing the phenomenon with a stereotype, but rather searches for the animal's unique qualities. This approach does not lead to fragmentation and multiplicity. Instead, it leads to the perception of diversity within unity, whereby the unique quality of each mammal is seen holistically within the context of other mammals.

A biology grounded in authentic wholeness can recognise the inner organic order in an animal in such a way that its individual features can be explained by the basic organisation of the animal itself. In short, the mammal explains itself.

Plant Life: Multiplication of Unity

Another fascinating example of the process of multiplication in unity occurs naturally in the life of plants. While we can obtain the same result artificially with the hologram by breaking the plate into fragments, every gardener is aware that plant cuttings, whether these be a branch, a twig or a stalk, result in the growth of an entirely new plant. The tendency for the whole plant to grow out of each portion of the original is striking. And certain plants, such as gloxinia and begonia, have the power to grow a complete new plant from each of their leaves – indicating that a whole plant is present in the growth of each single leaf into a plant.[37]

When a gardener divides a fuchsia plant into many pieces, each one will grow until it flowers, unless impaired by other circumstances. Bortoft notes that we are accustomed to seeing this as quite an ordinary result from the art or science of plant propagation. But actually we are witnessing something quite extraordinary – the intrinsic ability of a living organism to produce multiplicity in unity, which is the unity of wholeness. Thus, no matter how many times we divide the fuchsia plant, it remains whole.

It should be noted, however, that just as when we divide the hologram plate, it is always the original picture but never the same piece of glass; similarly, when we divide the plant, it is always the original plant but never the same specimen.

Perceiving the Whole

Modern science can only approach the whole as if it were a thing among things. Thus, the scientist tries to grasp the whole as an object for interrogation. So, it is that science today, by virtue of the method which is its hallmark, is left with a fragmented world of things which it must then try to put together.

In following Goethe's approach to scientific knowledge, one finds that the wholeness of the phenomenon is intensive. The experience is one of entering into a dimension which is in the phenomenon, not behind or beyond it, but which is not visible at first. It is perceived through the mind, when the mind functions as an organ of perception instead of the medium of logical thought. The experience of authentic wholeness requires a new style of learning, largely ignored in our schools and universities today.

In this chapter, we have briefly touched upon a few examples which illustrate the concept of wholeness. The *Ishopanishad* captures the indivisibility of the whole in a profound mantra:

पूर्णमदः पूर्णमिदं पूर्णात्पूर्णमुदच्यते।
पूर्णस्य पूर्णमादाय पूर्णमेवावशिष्यते।।

That (the macrocosm) is whole;
So is this (the microcosm) whole;
When whole is taken out of whole,
What remains is whole.

Chapter 17

DAVID BOHM: FROM RADICALISM TO WHOLENESS

David Bohm was born to a Hungarian Jewish immigrant father and a Lithuanian Jewish mother. He was raised mainly by his father, a furniture store owner and assistant of the local rabbi. Bohm graduated from Pennsylvania State College in 1939 and headed west to the California Institute of Technology for a year, after which he was transferred to the theoretical physics group under Robert Oppenheimer at the University of California, Berkeley, where he obtained his doctorate.

Bohm lived in the same neighbourhood as some of Oppenheimer's other graduate students, and as a group they became increasingly involved not only with physics but with radical politics. Bohm found a natural sympathy with alternative models of society, and he became active in such organisations as the Young Communist League, the Campus Committee to Fight Conscription, and the Committee for Peace Mobilization. These were all later branded as 'Communist organisations'.

During World War II, the Manhattan Project mobilised much of Berkeley's physics research in the effort to produce the first atomic bomb. Although Oppenheimer had asked Bohm to work with him at Los Alamos – the top-secret laboratory established in 1942 to design the bomb – the head of the Manhattan Project, General Leslie Groves, would not approve Bohm's security clearance after receiving tip-offs about his politics. In consequence, Bohm continued to teach physics at Berkeley until the completion of his PhD in 1943. 'The scattering calculations (of collisions of protons and deuterons) that he had completed proved useful to the Manhattan Project. Without security clearance, Bohm was denied access to his own work; not only would he be barred from defending his thesis, he was not even allowed to write his own thesis in the first place!'[38] To satisfy the university, Oppenheimer certified that Bohm had successfully completed the research.

After the war ended, Bohm became an assistant professor at Princeton University, where he worked closely with Albert Einstein. In May 1949, at the beginning of the McCarthyism period, the House Un-American Activities Committee called upon Bohm to testify before it. Bohm pleaded the Fifth Amendment right to decline to testify, and refused to give evidence against his colleagues. In 1950, he was charged with refusing to answer questions before the Committee and was arrested. He was acquitted in May 1951, by which time Princeton had already suspended him. After the acquittal, although Bohm's colleagues sought to have his position at Princeton reinstated and despite the fact that Einstein reportedly wanted Bohm to serve as his assistant, the university did not renew his contract. Bohm then, left for Brazil to take up a Chair in Physics at the University of São Paulo.

During this early period, Bohm made a number of significant contributions to physics, particularly in the area of quantum mechanics and relativity theory. His first book, *Quantum Theory*, published in 1951, was well-received (by Einstein among others). However, Bohm became dissatisfied with the orthodox approach to quantum theory and began to develop his own approach, which aligned with non-deterministic quantum theory.

In 1955, Bohm moved to Israel and spent two years there. It was here that he met Saral, who was to become his wife and an important figure in the development of his ideas. In 1957, they moved to the UK, where Bohm took up a research fellowship at the University of Bristol. In 1959, together with his student Yakir Aharonov, he discovered what became known as the 'Aharonov-Bohm effect'. This showed how an electro-magnetic field could affect a region of space in which the field had been shielded, even though its vector potential did exist there. Bohm was subsequently appointed Professor of Theoretical Physics at Birkbeck College, London, where his collected papers are preserved to this day.

'In 1959, his wife, Saral, recommended that he read the works of the Indian philosopher Jiddu Krishnamurti. Bohm was impressed by the way his own ideas on quantum mechanics meshed with the philosophical ideas of Krishnamurti. The two men met and went on to become close friends for over twenty five years, sharing a deep mutual interest in philosophy and the state of humanity.

Bohm was deeply interested in exploring the nature of reality – with the practical aim of finding a path to greater harmony through greater understanding. Having acknowledged that: 'The notion that reality is to be understood as process is an ancient one,'[39] Bohm concluded that reality is an 'unknown and indefinable totality of flux' which includes not only all matter but also the process of thought itself. He asked and answered his own rhetorical question, that if reality is unknown and unknowable, 'how can we be certain that it is there at all? The answer, of course, is that we can't be certain.'[40]

Then, how do things appear and, in their tangibility, have apparent solidity? Bohm explained it thus: 'Essentially, what is manifest… has its ground in the holomovement which is vast, rich, and in a state of unending flux of enfoldment and unfoldment… it cannot be grasped as something solid, tangible and stable to the senses (or to our instruments). Nevertheless… the overall law (holonomy) may be assumed to be such that in a certain sub-order, within the whole set of implicate order, there is totality of forms that have an approximate kind of recurrence, stability and separability. Evidently, these forms are capable of appearing as the relatively solid, tangible, and stable elements that makes up our manifest world.'[41]

Bohm also made significant theoretical contributions to neuropsychology and the development of the holonomic model of the functioning of the brain.

Importantly, Bohm believed that: 'Only a view of knowledge as an integral part of the total flux of process may lead generally to a more harmonious and orderly approach to life as a whole, rather than to a static and fragmentary view which does not treat knowledge as process, and which splits knowledge off from the rest of reality.'[42]

In his later years, Bohm wrote a proposal for a solution that has become known as the 'Bohm Dialogue', in which equal status and 'free space' form the most important prerequisites of communication and the appreciation of differing personal beliefs. His intention was to address societal problems, and his suggestion was that if these 'dialogue groups' were experienced on a sufficiently wide scale, they could help to overcome the isolation and fragmentation that he had observed to be inherent in society.

Bohm developed a comprehensive approach to the question of wholeness in science, society and the human thought process, which was presented in his outstanding work, *Wholeness and the Implicate Order*. He continued his work in quantum physics well past his academic retirement in 1987. His final works were posthumously published under the title, *The Undivided Universe: An Ontological Interpretation of Quantum Theory*.[43]

Chapter 18

LIVING ENERGIES AND NATURE

NOTES ON THE WORK OF VIKTOR SCHAUBERGER[44]

THE ORIGIN OF ENERGY

Viktor Schauberger began with the hypothesis that the original source of energy is a radiant emanation from what he described as the 'cause of causes', which he named the 'Eternally Creative Intelligence' or ECI. Since it is the cause of all causes, the ECI causes its own evolution constantly. Energy may, therefore, be viewed as an expression of ECI's 'will to create' – an agency through which the ideas of the ECI become manifest.

Radiating from the ECI, energy operates in the most sublime of realms, in all directions and to all parts of the unmanifested universe. Since it is limited neither by constraints of matter, the speed of light nor the conservation of energy law, it is present in all parts of the universe simultaneously. No conditions apply to it, and it does not exist for any specific purpose. It is pure, and can be freely employed either and equally for good or evil. From an originally undifferentiated state, the energetic entity becomes endowed with either a positive or negative charge and enters the lower worlds of duality.

By replacing the ECI with the sun – our principal source of life energy – one could say that the solar wind, which is actually waves of high energy particles, impinges on the earth's atmosphere. This creates turbulence in the form of air waves due to thermal and energetic reactions, which represent the first demodulation from a high energetic state to a motion of lower velocity and intensity. These reactions, in turn, generate waves of yet lower velocity but greater physicality on the surface of the ocean, which is a denser medium with more harmonically stabilised energy than air. Finally, the ocean waves form nearly static ripples in the sand on the ocean floor.

Schauberger states that the ECI is imbued with the desire to create and is constantly seeking new knowledge gained through the experiences of its multifarious creations in order to create an even better universe. As human beings, we could be construed as the creative, cellular organisms within the host entity of the ECI. These organisms contribute to its overall development, although we have no inkling of the spaces and higher planes in which the ECI operates. As a corollary, there is no absolute truth as such, however profound and absolute it may appear to be. Such a truth must move and develop with the evolution of its discoverer, the ECI. In almost nothing, is almost everything. Taken to its extreme, it could therefore be said that in nothing is everything; that all manifestation emerges through the 'eye of the needle', as it were, from the high potency, formless void of the ECI.

The amount of energy a human being requires for survival over one year is on an average 1000 kilowatt-hours (kWh). According to Viktor Schauberger's calculations, a human being operates at the relatively insignificant energy level of an electric light bulb, namely 100 watts. The average amount of energy received from the sun annually per square metre of ground surface is 1000kWh. Theoretically, therefore, all a human being needs to do is to stand in a square metre and obtain his/her energy from the sun. If we were able to transmute this energy directly, our energy requirement would be met, at least in terms of the amount of energy and oxygen required by a human being for the maintenance of bodily functions, reproduction, creativity and intelligent thought for a whole year.

Conversely, the average petrol consumption of a car with a 1.6 litre engine amounts to between ten and eleven litres per 100 km. Schauberger calculated that to travel a distance of 1000 km requires an energy expenditure of 1000 kWh. This highlights the ludicrous mechanical efficiency we have so far managed to achieve and of which we are so proud. In short, a car travelling 1000 km destructively consumes the same amount of energy in a few hours that a human being uses far more economically and productively over a whole year. And the car does not think, it does not reproduce, nor is it creative; it has no such abilities. Equating 1000 km travelled with the annual activity of one human being produces a very poor energy relationship.

The amount of oxygen used by a human being in a year is 260 kg. To drive a car at 50 km an hour requires 22.25 kg of oxygen per hour, which is roughly 750 times the amount needed by a human being. Therefore, as we drive happily along in our cars, we unknowingly take 750 oxygen-breathing slaves along with us. These slaves, however, do not breathe out nice, healthy carbon-dioxide and water as we do, but they spew out a noxious concoction of poisonous gases. In a journey lasting eleven hours, all the oxygen required by one human being for one year has been consumed by the vehicle. The relationship between our technology and its use of energy is diametrically opposed to that of nature.

The Dislocation of Nature and Humanity

As the human population has grown and a technology based on 'modern' science has gradually developed, the paths of nature and of 'modern' technology have begun to diverge. In the last 150 years or so, the advances and application of technology have accelerated enormously and, consequently, the divergence has become dramatic. The subtle energy systems of nature have been overwhelmed by the ceaseless onslaught of a merciless, mechanistic technology, with direct consequences for us all. We are presented today with an extremely fateful choice: we can either choose life or ultimate oblivion.

All motion resolves itself into more and more physically material, self-contained units through the increase in encircling rotational velocity. This leads to an increasing manifestation of 'illusory' material substance. The greater and tighter the encirclement of space, the more physical the apparent matter becomes and the greater the degree of attachment.

For evolution to proceed, nature increases her capital by, say ten per cent, in terms of growth, movement and the evolution of new life forms. Human beings should, therefore, learn to live off the surplus of nature's interest on her own capital. This is probably quite ample for our needs. With such a system, stability would increase because increasing diversity means more legs to stand on, so to speak. If one leg is accidentally removed, the whole system does not collapse. The natural system is, and has ever been, sustainable.

We are imprisoned today, in an energy system which is self-annihilating. Since we cannot actually see energy itself but only its outward manifestation, its origins may well lie in a reality beyond our senses. Perhaps energy is the culmination of a desire to create, to afford every possibility for the gaining of new experience. While there are many energies of which science is aware and has subjected to measurement, there are other forms of energy of which we are aware but which defy all scientific quantification, since they are too subtle to be detected even by the most sophisticated scientific instruments.

Examples include various human energies such as thought, desire, love, enthusiasm and aggression, which are emanations from the human psyche and motivators for action. While science may be able to detect brain activity related to these phenomena, it cannot actually measure their intrinsic power, size, frequency or vibrational state, nor their true point of origin. 'That day is fast approaching when it will be confessed that the "forces" we know of are but the phenomenal manifestations of realities we know nothing about, but which were known to the ancients and by them worshipped.'[46]

The 'Will to Create'

Viktor Schauberger maintained that any given phenomenon always has its counterpart or counter-aspect, and both components should always be taken into account. The manifestation of all natural forces is the result of the interaction between two opposites, neither of which ever reaches totality in the lower realms of duality (the physical world), for they can only become total when they unite within their unifying, non-physical, governing principle.

All physical manifestation develops as the product of focused energy emanating from a seed of desire, of Schauberger's 'will to create'. This manifests as vibrations carrying the image or the idea of that which is to be created. That form (and that form only) can then arise. It corresponds faithfully to the idea of the thing itself or, in other words, to the particular pattern of vibrations.

Resonance is the free transfer of energy or the sympathetic vibration between one stem and another without any loss of energy. It is the function of mutually harmonically related frequencies. The quantitative thrust of modern technology and ideology is pressing downwards towards uniformity, to a vibrationless state, which is equivalent to zero energy and quality. Thus, species after species is disappearing simply because the ambient creative energetic matrix, which has to do with upward evolution, has been rendered inoperative. It appears that all we have left now is all that we can still preserve. Viktor suspected that the point may have already been reached where existing areas of forest and vegetation are insufficient to compensate for what is presently being consumed, thus creating a net oxygen deficit.

Higher spirituality is synonymous with a higher level of energy. As the will to create intensifies, the forces become more concentrated, extraneous elements are ejected and a channel is opened to the free passage of creative energy. This results in an increasing charge (life-force), energetic density and rotational velocity. A vortex of life energy evolves, into which more and higher qualities of energy are drawn for the generation and development of the form itself.

All motion becomes directional, radiant and universal through decreased rotational motion. It is the all-important 'letting go' of disengagement or detachment. The development of a pure love untrammelled by attachment or other hindrances, for example, slowly increases its power and radiates more and more.

Schauberger asserted that the human body could be seen as a hollow energy path, a complex toroidal vortex for the transmutation of the energy of matter into physical and intellectual activity. Everything we see around us – trees, flowers, buildings – are all the outside casing of the formative energy path. While the main body of a tree's energy lies above it, the tree can only grow to a certain height because the energies are only able to draw up the physical mass of the tree so far in their wake. For us to be able to create a sustainable and viable society, it is necessary to deepen our understanding of all the processes of natural motion and temperature, and of the vital relationship between trees, water and soil productivity.

Nature's workings can be described not as 'wheels within wheels' but as 'whorls within whorls'. It is all the more extraordinary, therefore, that despite so much evidence of this vortical, cyclical, helical movement, which lies everywhere in Nature before our very eyes, science has never ascribed any fundamental importance to it or tried to copy it. It has been too immersed in the Euclidean elements of mechanics with little knowledge or conceptions of organics.

Water, the Carrier of Life

Comprehension of the sublime energetic interdependencies upon which life at all its levels is founded is of profound significance. Viktor Schauberger saw the whole earth as an organism, and he perceived water to be the carrier of life, the ultimate source of what we call 'consciousness'. He saw how running water attracts the human consciousness like a magnet and draws a small part of it along with it. This force can act so powerfully that we temporarily lose our consciousness and involuntarily fall asleep. Schauberger examined in depth some fascinating questions pertaining to the movement of water. These include: why does the groundwater in wells rise far above the surface of the ground? Why don't wooden posts rot under water, but only above it? Why can rising cold water pierce through the hardest rock? Why does water pulsate and breathe? Why does groundwater manage to remain on the sides of mountains? Why, growing colder and heavier, does it rise, and why does it frequently spring from high peaks?

He also examined why west-to-east flowing watercourses fertilise their banks while the banks of east-to-west flowing rivers are barren, and why the banks of south-to-north flowing watercourses are fertile on one side only; why rivers flowing into cold seas migrate laterally to the north; why deltas and estuaries develop; and why a trout stands still in a raging torrent, as if by magic.

And, looking at the sea, he wondered: why is the water at the poles warmer at the bottom? Why is the sunlit surface at the poles so icily cold? Why doesn't the warmer, lighter base-water of the seas rise? Why are the water temperatures at the Equator so warm? Why does water get colder with increasing depth and yet warmer again below the boundary layer of +4°C? Why does life below this boundary layer begin anew? Why does the salt content of the seas vary? Why do herrings migrate northwards in water? And why do deep sea fish glow? He was equally intrigued by the following conundrum: why the warm Gulf Stream pushes the cold sea water aside and wends its way for thousands of kilometres over mountains and valleys in a reversed temperature gradient, without the assistance of a mechanical gradient.

In contrast to currently held doctrines, Nature is founded far more on co-operation than on competition, because it is only through harmonious interplay that physical formation can occur, that things can come together and structures can be built up. Without an attraction between two or more atoms, there would be no water, no plants, no chemical compounds, no living substances at all. In essence, attraction is a form of love, so that in the polygamous relationship between two hydrogen atoms and one oxygen atom, their mutual attraction and interaction gives birth to the marvel of water.

Water is the issue most crucial to all life on earth. Water is the life-blood of our planet, the life-giving fluid in all organisms, plants, animals and human beings alike, flowing as sap, lymph or blood; our very existence is therefore, intimately connected with the quality of water available to us. It is vital for our own lives and those of our children that we should become seriously concerned not only for the health, vitality and quality of the water we drink, but also for its original source and the treatment it receives. Apart from our own consumption of it, this same water is also used to grow everything we eat. If we want to live in health and happiness, then the living entity – water – should be highly revered and the most sensitive care taken of it.

Envisioning the Future

Viktor Schauberger's overriding desire was to provide present and future generations with the ability in terms of knowledge and machines with which to usher in and sustain a golden age of prosperity, peace and harmony. He wished to furnish those who would protect or save life with an energy source that could produce energy so cheaply that nuclear fission would not only be proven to be uneconomical, but ridiculous. However, he was apprehensive, because he believed that if he revealed everything he knew about the natural energies of the planet, his information would 'only be hushed up, because it not only involved the whole scientific establishment, but also the doctrines of the Church.'[47]

He believed – and demonstrated – that an energy concept in accord with nature's processes could be realised and could provide the generation virtually free energy. But he knew that the pursuit of profit and power for its own sake, coupled with the necessary systems of control, had relegated the mass of humanity to a state of almost total dependency for everything it needs in the way of food, energy, health and all other necessities of life. Indeed, there are many cases where significant improvements in energy generation, health treatment and agricultural productivity (to name but a few) have been suppressed in favour of the vested interests of those whose natural humanitarian sensibilities have been corrupted by the lust for power and material gain.

Viktor believed that control over the systems of energy was at the forefront of this battle. The present lamentable condition of the planet – our only home in this vast universe – has now reached such a parlous state that for our own survival we simply cannot afford to allow present methods of energy exploitation to continue. It is becoming more and more clearly evident that we need to change our ways and practices drastically if we are to survive as a race. If it is to remain at the cutting edge of human endeavour, science too, as a leading influence on human thought and activity, will have to raise its visions and thinking one octave higher. In the process it will, perhaps, begin to appreciate its lack of omniscience, and approach matters with a far greater humility than it has to date.

As a vital first step, the development of a new technology – an eco-technology – harmonious and conforming to Nature's laws, is imperative and will demand a radical and fundamental change in our way of thinking and our approach to the interpretation of the established doctrines and facts of physics, chemistry, agriculture, forestry and water management.

NOTES

1. Henri Bortoft, 1996, *The Wholeness of Nature: Goethe's Way of Science*, Floris Books, Edinburgh, UK, p.17.
2. *ibid* p.17.
3. *ibid* p.xi.
4. Callum Coats, 2001, *Living Energies, An Exposition of Concepts Related to the Theories of Viktor Schauberger*, p.6.
5. *ibid* p.6.
6. *ibid* p.6.
7. Jeremy Naydler (ed.), 1996, *Goethe on Science: An Anthology of Goethe's Scientific Writings*, p.124.
8. *ibid* p.37.
9. *ibid* p.12.
10. *ibid* p.19.
11. *ibid* p.21.
12. *ibid* p.23.
13. *ibid* p.23.
14. *ibid* p.27.
15. *ibid* p.28.
16. *ibid* p.28.
17. *ibid* p.50.
18. *ibid* p.33.
19. *ibid* p.34.
20. *ibid* p.34.
21. *ibid* p.36.
22. *ibid* p.52.
23. The author's guru, Pandit Motilal Shastri, and his guru, Pandit Madhusudan Ojha, defined the process of knowing how one becomes many as *vijnana*, and realising and experiencing oneness in multiplicity as *jnana*.
24. Jeremy Naydler, *op cit*, p.60.
25. *ibid* p.92.
26. *ibid* p.66.
27. *ibid* p.64.
28. Henri Bortoft, *op cit*, p.56.
29. *ibid* p.57.
30. *ibid* p.92.
31. *ibid* p.125.
32. A poem by Goethe, quoted in Norbert Elias, 2001, *The Society of Individuals*, p.66.
33. This chapter is excerpted from Henri Bortoft, *op cit*.
34. *ibid* p.4.
35. *ibid* p.5.
36. Wolfgang Schad, 1977, *Man and Mammals: Toward a Biology of Form*.
37. Henri Bortoft, *op cit,* p.256.
38. F David Peat, 1997, *Infinite Potential: The Life and Times of David Bohm*.
39. David Bohm, 1980, *Wholeness and the Implicate Order*, p.48.
40. *ibid* p.59.

41. *ibid* p.184.
42. *ibid* p.63.
43. David Bohm, 1993 (posthumous work), *The Undivided Universe: An ontological interpretation of quantum theory*.
44. This chapter consists of extracts from the book, *Living Energies, An Exposition of Concepts Related to the Theories of Viktor Schauberger* by Callum Coats. RK Mishra intended to use these excerpts as background information for his own chapter on Schauberger's important contribution to human understanding. Sadly, this was not accomplished in the author's lifetime. It is hoped that the notes which comprise this chapter will inspire readers to study Schauberger's works in depth. We extend our full acknowledgment and gratitude to Callum Coats for his thorough explication of the work of Schauberger.
46. *ibid* p.37.
47. *ibid* p.13.

SECTION SEVEN

~

THE WORKINGS OF WHOLENESS IN OUR WORLD

Chapter 19

SOUND AND COMMUNICATION

Let us begin our exploration into the profound subject of sound, word and meaning by acknowledging the all-pervasiveness and power of sound. The Upanishads state that in the beginning there was only sound, and everything came into existence from that sound. Even modern scientists are beginning to recognise that a vibration reverberates ceaselessly throughout the cosmos, underlying all matter and forming the substratum of everything. Just as it pulsates within all objects in the universe, it also pulsates within us.[1]

In essence, sound is the foundation of our awareness, and as such is synonymous with our identity. It is the expression of the consciousness of an individual, and is present both within and outside the body. Bereft of sound, a sentient person loses consciousness. Sound is the basic source of life that stimulates a person to remain engaged in his or her activities. To put it another way, sound distinguishes a sentient person from an insentient. Whether it is the reading of a person's pulse, the heartbeat, or the inhaling and exhaling of the breath – sound is common to all. Knowledge of arts or science, form and content captured in words are all manifestations of sound in various forms.

The Unceasing Resonance of Sound

The all-pervasiveness of sound can be noticed in matters profound as well as mundane. Whether we are working in an office or in a factory, whether we are cooking or cleaning, whether we are working by hand or by pen, we create sound.

Shabda or sound never disappears. We prefer to use the Sanskrit term 'shabda' here because its English equivalent does not convey the full flavour of the original term. The 'word' or shabda is a manifestation of sound. It emanates from *akasha*, the first of the five gross material elements. The commencement of every action, practice, motion, state, birth, existence or demise is invariably associated with the manifestation of sound in some form. The 'desire' or 'intention' to undertake or launch an activity manifests itself as shabda in the mind; the desire to 'do' stimulates the impulse to articulate the desire and express it in words.

Even when we are sitting quietly, the inhaling and exhaling of the breath generate a subtle imperceptible shabda or sound. A long deep breath is, of course, audible at a distance. In fact, the knowledge of the ideal breathing technique can keep several diseases and disorders away which often afflict the human body. The entire universe is resonating with life-giving waves of the energy of sound. Within our body, the heartbeat constitutes a critical form of sound. The air that flows in space, and which the universe 'breathes', never ceases but pulsates with sound endlessly. Rivers sing and oceans roar. Even when we turn a small screw, sound emanates. Sound is produced by vehicles, boats and aeroplanes. It is easy to imagine how much sound the movement of the earth must be producing. Sound permeates numerous universes, suns, moons and multiverses.

Shabda is pure light. It is spontaneous and original. The light that we commonly use is derived and distorted; but all of us experience at one time or another the light that shines in our hearts. The light of word is similar to this. It exists as numerous particles of sound, which are subtle and normally not discernible. When we attempt to speak, these numerous particles of shabda aggregate in a word or a sentence to communicate the meaning, emotions or idea.

Shabda is perceived as a unit of language. In ordinary parlance, people may use it to mean sound or word. Shabda is that which, when articulated, is seen to convey the idea of the referent. It is the cause that produces the idea of its meaning. We may call it, therefore, the 'meaning bearer'. The articulated sound, or the phoneme or the word or the sentence is that which we refer to as 'shabda'.

Shabda is used to suggest both a word and a sentence, and comprises two aspects – form and content. Some view this relationship between the two as a cause and effect relationship, while others hold that the two are intertwined. Still others assert that the two are identical. On deeper observation, we find that a word is like a piece of wood in which fire remains unmanifest. It becomes manifest when this piece is rubbed with another piece of wood. Before speaking, we have already thought what we have to say; that thought is related to the word and becomes meaning.

All material objects require some space to 'keep' them and they have to be seen in sequence to understand them.

For example, if you want to read a book you go through its pages one by one, sentence by sentence, word by word. This applies to all 'individuals', whether they be solid, liquid or gaseous. The process of knowing them exists at a gross level and is time-consuming. But the process of knowing sound is exciting, in the sense that we can discern different sounds at the same time. If we are sitting in a railway carriage, for example, which is causing a lot of noise as it moves; within that carriage there may be a group of people who are sitting together, talking, gossiping, maybe singing, perhaps writing. In all of these activities, even if they are sitting quietly reading a book, they are creating sound. And we are able to relate to all these various types of sounds simultaneously.

Similarly, each instrument in an orchestra generates its specific sound, yet none of the sounds flowing from the different instruments obstructs the flow of the sound from the other instruments. In fact, these are mutually supportive and reinforcing, so that the music which emanates is a melody of the various sounds.

When we engage in conversation, we create word 'pictures' made of sound particles. Only a few words are needed to translate the picture that is in our mind, transform it into sounds and communicate the same to the listener. As soon as a word is uttered, these subtle sound particles aggregate and give a vast quality to the meaning of the word.

In the minutest corner of the brain, virtually the entire universe is captured. In that small portion are located pictures of mountains and rivers, oceans and countries, sentient and insentient beings, houses and palaces, trees and plants, songs and dances. When we are engaged in conversation, the pictures forwarded in our mind float before our eyes as if we were witnessing a cinema show. But of course, these are not films; they are pictures made of subtle elements of sound. As soon as the word is uttered, these subtle 'atoms' of sound paint a picture.

Sound also has an effect on the quality of a structure, organic or otherwise, and this fact is reflected subconsciously in language. For instance, we say that a structure is 'sound' or 'unsound', meaning that it is either safe or unsafe. Similarly, a person is said to be of 'sound' or 'unsound' mind, reflecting her or his creative or destructive propensities.

The Wholeness of Communication

All knowledge is captured and expressed in words. Language is comprised of words and, as we know, it is language which differentiates human beings from other species. While it is true that human beings communicate with each other through various means (such as body language and touch), the most obvious and widely recognised form of communication is the spoken word. (Silence, too, is a form of communication, which is developed as a part of various systems of meditation.)

Let us go a little deeper now. Speech is a product of sound and consists of words. In fact, before we utter a single word, the ideas that we are going to communicate through that word take shape in our mind. And before those ideas take concrete shape in the mind, a process begins at a deeper level where the ideas are still in a diffused state but have already started taking shape. Going deeper we reach, as it were, the source where all thoughts and ideas lie in an unmanifest state. From that source, where the 'seed' lies hidden, the process of 'sprouting' an idea or a thought commences. It spreads out like a diffused cloud, then coalesces into an idea and bursts forth as 'rain' – the articulated speech which seeks to communicate the idea to the listener.

Speech is of four types. We are conversant with the normal speech that we use in daily interactions. But that speech which we actually utter is only a small part of the process, perhaps one-fourth of our potential. We see only the idea and its articulation. Speech actually begins with a state of wholeness. At the source, there is total identity between word and the idea it communicates. The process of separation starts at the second phase; this is followed by the process of concretisation of an idea at the third stage; and it culminates in its articulation from the mouth as it travels to the listener, at the fourth stage.

Every word or sentence contains ideas and emotions, and in that sense we paint a 'word picture' of an idea or thought in our mind. Speech then acts like a flash of light, which communicates the word picture containing those emotions and ideas. This is known as *sphota*. It is as if a camera has captured a thought in the mind and then articulated the same to the outside world in the form of 'pictures' made of words and sentences. The communication of an idea to a listener creates the impression of the thought being separate from the language in which it is stored. Without understanding the relationship between the idea that emanates in the mind and the words in which it is communicated to the listener, it is impossible to understand the principles of linguistics or the modes of human communication.

The relationship between language and the ideas, objects or thoughts it contains and communicates is like that of the body and the life-force (prana) that sustains it. The function of sphota is to arrange the undifferentiated sound in words and sentences and to give them meaning. Words are not independent entities communicating meaning from their own side. Rather, the meaning provides content which, in turn, is organised in the form of language at a deeper level. Thus, we see that words and meaning are not two different entities.

Sphota may be described as the transcendent ground in which the spoken syllables and conveyed meaning find themselves united as word or shabda. The original conception of sphota seems to date back to the Vedic period. Sphota is the permanent element in the word and may be considered the essence of the word; *dhwani* – the uttered sounds – are the actualised and ephemeral elements and are an aspect of the sphota. The external aspect of sphota is the uttered sound (or written word) perceived by our sense organs, which serves merely to manifest the inner sphota with its inherent word meaning.

At first, the word exists in the mind of the speaker as a unity or sphota. When we utter it, we produce a sequence of different sounds which appear to have a differentiation between them. The listener, although first hearing a series of sounds, ultimately perceives the utterance as a unity – the same sphota with which the speaker began – and then meaning is conveyed.

Just as an object reflected in water may seem to have movement because of the water's movement, so does the word or sphota takes on the properties of uttered speech (sequence, loudness or softness, accent and so on) in which it is manifested. The question may arise as to why this changeless whole or sphota should ever come to be expressed in the phenomenal diversity called language. Such phenomenalisation occurs because the sphota itself contains an inner energy which seeks to burst forth into expression. Then the unitary sphota is seen to contain all the potentialities for diversity.

Even though the sphota theory envisages different subdivisions of the sphota, the famous philosopher of Sanskrit grammar, Bhartrahari, accepts only the sentence sphota as the real unit of speech. Letters and words have a mere pragmatic value as useful units which build up higher units of speech, such as the sentence. The meaning of this single, indivisible utterance is *pratibha*, a flash of insight, the real nature of which is indefinable. Its existence is ratified only in the individual's experience of it, and the experiencer is unable to describe it adequately.[2]

The Power of Mantras

As a form of energy, sound has long been attributed a form-creating capacity. Prayers, chanting, Indian ragas and the uttering of mantras are believed to produce various effects, some of which are concrete in form.

The Vedas were articulated as mantras by seer-scientists endowed with deep insights and powerful intuition. As the meaning of the mantras were unravelled, these *rishis* visualised the nature of the universe. The mantras were revealed to them, and they had a clear perception of the ideas they contained. The mantras spontaneously poured out of the hearts of the seer-scientists and became known by different designations. However, the entirety of their knowledge is encapsulated within the term 'mantra' itself;

its meaning is 'sound', and sound reverberates in everything in this universe.[3]

Mantras are not merely aggregations of sounds, but a special aspect of consciousness which unites a letter with the energy that flows from universal consciousness. This energy is visualised as being feminine. Normally latent, she is likened to a sleeping serpent coiled round the spark of light concealed in the heart of every person. And this coiled serpent straightens when the spark of meditation is concentrated on her.

The energy of universal consciousness is continuously and effortlessly invested in words. When that energy is absent, collections of words are like a mass of clouds in the rainless autumn sky, bereft of power. It is consciousness that invests mantras with life. Mantras are collections of words endowed with the power of the letters of the alphabet. Imbued with supraphysical energy, they are powerful vehicles for the attainment of knowledge.

Mantras are all composed of letters endowed with the supreme energy, and they exude supreme light which fills the universe. Consonants in Sanskrit become alive when 'a', the primordial vowel, joins them. This light spreads out everywhere as the letter 'a' embraces every other letter. The indestructible energy flowing from infinite universal consciousness is the life of mantras; for mantras cannot exist separately from their inherent energy.

We present here a note on the Sanskrit alphabet for the benefit of those of our readers who are unfamiliar with the Sanskrit language. This section aims to introduce the principles underlying the concept of the power of the Sanskrit alphabet, and of its words and mantras. Firstly, here is a guide to the letters of the alphabet with their rendering in English:

Key to Transliteration

Vowels					
अ a	आ *ā*	इ *i*	ई *īd*	उ *u*	ऊ *ū*
(but)	(palm)	(it)	(beet)	(put)	(pool)
ऋ *ṛ*	ए *e*	ऐ *ai*	ओ *o*	औ *au*	
(rhythm)	(play)	(air)	(toe)	(loud)	
CONSONANTS					
Guttural	क ka	ख* kha	ग ga	घ gha	ङ ṅa
	(skarte)	(blockhead)	(gate)	(ghost)	(sing)
Palatal	च ca	छ* cha	ज ja	झ jha	ञ ña
	(chunk)	(catch him)	(john)	(hedgehog)	(bunca)
Lingual	ट ṭa	ठ ṭha	ड ḍa	ढ ḍha	ण* ṇa
	(start)	(anthill)	(dart)	(godhead)	(under)
Dental	त ta	थ tha	द da	ध dha	न na
	(path)	(thunder)	(that)	(breathe)	(numb)
Labial	प pa	फ pha	ब ba	भ bha	म ma
	(spin)	(philosophy)	(bin)	(abhor)	(much)
Others	य *ya*	र *ra*	ल *la*	व *va*	
	(young)	(drama)	(luck)	(vile)	
	श *śa*	ष *ṣh*	स *sa*	ह *ha*	
	(shove)	(bushel)	(so)	(hum)	
	क्ष *kṣa*	त्र *tra*	ज्ञ *jña*	ळ* *ḷ*	ॠ *ṝ*
	(ksatriya)	*(trishūl)*	*(jñani)*	*(play)*	

अं (—)ṁ anusvāra (nasalisation of preceding vowel) like *saṁkṛti*

अः ḥ (*prātaḥ*) ḥ *visarga* (aspiration of preceding vowel)

ऽ 'Avagraha' consonant # consonant (like:- *ime 'vasthitā*)

Anusvāra at the end of line is presented by म् = m (not ṁ)

HINDI LETTER (Extras)

ँ ñ	ं ṇ	ड़* ṛa	ढ़* ṛha
(Candrabindu)	(anusvāara)		

* No exact English equivalents for these letters.

The following is a guide to the pronunciation of the letters of the Sanskrit alphabet.

VOWELS

Sanskrit vowels are categorised as either long or short. In English translation, the long vowels are indicated with a macron – a horizontal line over the vowel – with the exception of the *e* and the ai, and the *o* and the *au*, which are always long.

Short	Long	
a as in cup	*a* as in father	*ai* as in aisle
i as in give	*e* as in save	*au* as in cow
u as in full	*i* as in seen	*u* as in school
	o as in know	

CONSONANTS

The main differences between Sanskrit and English pronunciation of consonants are in the aspirated and retroflexive letters. The aspirated letters have a definite *h* sound. The Sanskrit letter *kh* is pronounced as in inkhorn; the *th* as in boathouse; the *ph* as in loophole. The retroflexes are pronounced with the tip of the tongue touching the hard palate; *t*, for instance, is pronounced as in ant; *d* as in end. The sibilants are *s'*, *s*, and *s*. The *s* is pronounced as *sh* but with the tongue touching the soft palate; the *s* as *sh* with the tongue touching the hard palate; the *s* as in history. Double consonants take an extra emphasis. Other distinctive consonants are these:

c as in church
ch as in pitch-hook
n as in canyon
m is a strong nasal
h is a strong aspiration

The following paragraphs are intended to give readers a flavour of the rigorous scientific basis for the grammar and the science of words in Sanskrit. Some understanding of these factors helps us to appreciate the principles underlying the concept of the power of letters of the Sanskrit alphabet.

Panini renders the science of words (grammar and philology) in aphorisms or sutras in his seminal work *Ashtadhyayi* ('Eight Chapters'), and these are of six kinds: (a) a definition, (b) the key to interpretation, (c) the statement of general rule, (d) a head or governing rule, which exerts a directing or governing influence over other rules, (e) extended application by analogy, (f) to communicate or make anything known by science[4]. Fourteen aphorisms contain the arrangement of the letters of the Sanskrit alphabet for grammatical purposes.

A grammatical symbol or abbreviation is formed by taking any letter which is not a non-efficient letter and joining it with any non-efficient letter that follows it. Thus, there is a symbol for all the vowels, all the consonants, all soft unaspirated consonants and all hard unaspirated consonants.

Principles of Pronunciation

Conjunct consonants are those consonants between which there is no heterogeneous separating vowel and which are pronounced jointly. That which is pronounced by the nose and mouth is called nasal (*anunasika*). Thus, the nasals are pronounced from two organs or places – the nose and the mouth. The pure nasal is known as *anusvara.* The difference between anusvara and anunasika lies in the fact that, in the latter, the breath passes through the nose and the mouth during pronunciation. If, instead of emitting the vowel sound freely through the mouth, we allow the velum pendulum to drop and the air to vibrate through the cavities which connect the nose with the pharynx, we hear the nasal vowels (anunasika).

Where the utterance and effort are equal, we have what are known as homogeneous letters. The chief places or parts of the mouth which are instrumental in the production of various sounds are the following: throat, palate, head, teeth, lips and nose.

The quality or effort expended in producing sound is of two sorts: 'internal' and 'external'. The first of these is subdivided into five parts:

1) Complete contact of the organs: twenty-five letters belong to this class. In pronouncing these, there is complete contact between the root of the tongue and various places such as the throat, palate, dome of the palate, teeth and lips.
2) Slight contact: in pronouncing these semi-vowels, the active and passive are necessary for the production of all consonantal sound, yet they may only approach each other and are not permitted to actually touch.
3) Complete opening: the vowels belong to this class.
4) Slight opening: some letters belong to this class.
5) Contracted letters: in actual usage, the organ in the enunciation of these letters is contracted but it is considered to be open – as in the case of the other vowels – only when the vowel is taking part in some operation of grammar.

All letters are divided in accordance with internal or external effort. The internal effort is the mode of articulation preparatory to the utterance of the sound, while the external effort is the mode of articulation at the close of the utterance of the sound. The division of letters according to internal effort gives us two mute letters, two semi-vowel or liquid letters, three vowels and four sibilants or flatus letters. The division of letters according to external efforts gives us surds (voiceless consonants), or *aghosha* letters, and consonants, or *ghosha* letters. The aghoshas are also known as *svdsa* letters and the ghoshas are known as *nada* letters. The second division of letters according to external effort is into aspirated and unaspirated.

The vowel has eighteen forms. Whether the vowels are acute, grave or circumflexed, each may be nasalised or not, and each of these six may be short, long or prolated.

Homogeneous (*savarna*) letters must satisfy two conditions: firstly, their place of pronunciation must be the same; and secondly, their quality must be equal. If one of these conditions is present but the other is absent, there can be no homogeneity.

This defines pronominals (*sarvanama*). All the rest are called pronouns. To correctly identify pronouns, we must refer to Panini's *Ganapatha* wherein a list of all groups, referred to in the aphorisms covering pronouns, is given.

The words prior (*poorva*), after (*paschaat*), posterior (*ananth*), south (*dakshina*), north (*uttara*), other (*apara*), and inferior (*adgara*) are optionally pronouns when they discriminate relative positions, but not when they are appellatives.

Seven words mentioned in the list of pronouns are always pronouns, when they have the meaning given to them in the list above – that is, when they imply a relation in time and space. But when they are used in any other sense than the one which has been determined or fixed for them, they are not pronouns; nor are they so when they are used as appellatives.

All affixes for the formation of nouns are of two kinds: there are those by which nouns are derived directly from roots, known as primary affixes; then there are those by which nouns are derived from other nouns, known as secondary affixes.

The adverbial or indeclinable compounds are formed by joining an indeclinable particle with another word. The resulting compound – in which the indeclinable particle generally forms the first element – is again indeclinable and usually ends, like adverbs, in the ordinary terminations of the nominative or accusative neuter.

In Sanskrit, there are twenty-one case-terminations, as arranged below:

		Singular	Dual	Plural
Nominative	★	★	★	★
Accusative	★	★	★	★
Instrumental	★	★	★	★
Dative	★	★	★	★
Ablative	★	★	★	★
Genitive	★	★	★	★
Locative	★	★	★	★

One aphorism in the sutras of Panini explains the mode of interpreting words used in the possessive case (sixth case). The genitive case (*shashthi*) denotes several sorts of relations in Sanskrit, such as causation, possession, relation in place, comparison, nearness, proximity, change, collection, component member, and so forth. When a word is used in the genitive case in an aphorism, doubt may arise as to the sense in which that genitive is to be used. One of the aphorisms lays down the restrictive rule for the interpretation of such words.

The Wheel of the Alphabet

The sixteen vowels – beginning with the form *a* and ending in *h* (*visarga*) – represent Shiva, the repository of the thirty-six *tattwas*. The five energies – of consciousness, bliss, will, knowledge and action – combine to constitute the Shiva tattwa.

The Sanskrit letters *a* and *ā* – which are one – are filled with the five energies. From the first two – the energies of consciousness and of bliss – arise the five consonants of *ka, kha, ga, gha* and *ria*. These five represent the states of the five gross elements: earth, water, fire, air and space. From the energy of will represented by the letters *i* and *ī*, five consonants arise, which are *ca, cha, ja, jha* and *na*. These five represent the states of the five subtle sense capacities (*tanmatras*): smell, taste, form, touch and sound. The two letters *ri* and *riī*, along with the five energies, give rise to the five consonants of *ta, tha, da, dha* and *na*. These consonants represent the five organs of action. The five consonants *ta, tha, da, dha* and *na*, which represent the five organs of knowledge, are produced by the same five energies through the letters *lri*, and *lrī*. The energy of knowledge, the letters *u* and *ū* and the five energies together, give rise to the five consonants of *pa, pha, ba, bha* and *ma*, and these produce the five elements of mind (mana), intellect (buddhi), ego (*ahamkara*), nature (*prakriti*), and the fundamental tattwa residing in the body of an individual (*purusha*). From earth to purusha there are twenty-five elements, because five energies exist in each energy of Shiva. Thus, the energies of consciousness, bliss, will, knowledge and action are intertwined.

The next four semi-vowels of *ya, ra, la,* and *va* correspond to the six elements known as the six 'coverings'. The 'blooming' of the self is represented by the four letters *sa*, *sa*, *sa* and *ha*. Shiva Shakti – the spontaneous energy of Shiva – is represented by the letter *ha*.

This, in essence, is the theory of the 'wheel of the alphabet' or *matrikachakram*. There are three worlds in this wheel: the subjective, cognitive and objective world. We, human beings, are situated in the objective world, and normally we are unaware of the cognitive or subjective worlds. But once an individual internalises the reality of this wheel, whatever (s)he does and whatever (s)he says will be filled with the supreme universal consciousness of 'I'. So how can we unite the objective and subjective worlds? The subjective world is found in *'a'* and the objective world is found in *'ha'*. In other words, Shakti is found in Shiva and Shiva is found in Shakti.

'*a-i-u*' is the first aphorism (sutra) of Panini's grammar. From these three letters – *a-i-u* – all other letters are produced. The letter *ā* rises from the letter *a* and so on, until the flow of visarga arises. And from that visarga, the letters from *ka* to *sa* arise.

The fifty letters listed above represent the existence of the whole universe. The universe is composed of thirty-six elements, and these are represented by the fifty letters.

In summary, the unparalleled state of consciousness is represented by the first letter in the Sanskrit alphabet, the letter *a*. The blissful state (ananda) is represented by the second letter in the Sanskrit alphabet, the letter ***a***. Two more movements follow. In the world of vowels, the subtle state of the will is represented by the letter *i*. The next vowel, signifying the gross state of will, is represented by the letter *i*. After that comes another movement, which is knowledge, and this is represented by the letter *u*. The next movement comprises the desire to observe the differentiated realities existing in Shiva's own nature, which is represented by the letter *u*. There are two additional movements in this process, represented by the letters *Iri* and *Irī*. Shiva's energy of action is represented by four letters: *e*, *ai*, *o* and *au*. The energy of action which is not yet vivid is represented by the letter *e*, and in its vivid state, it is represented by the letter *ai*. When it becomes even more vivid, it is represented by the letter *o*; and at its most vivid, it is represented by the letter *au*. The final state of the energy of action, represented by the letter *au*, will be found only in the universal state when the three energies of will, knowledge and action are fused into one universal point. This is visarga.

As noted earlier, Shiva has five energies: the energy of consciousness, bliss, will, knowledge and action. In each of these five energies, the other four are subsumed. Thus, all five forms of energy exist in each and every energy of Shiva. When the supreme energy of Shiva – supreme transcendental speech – descends to the field of the universe, it first becomes will, then knowledge and then action. Thereafter, it assumes the form of vowels, consonants, classes of letters, and holders of the classes of letters. In the Sanskrit alphabet, the vowels are one class of letters, and there are eight classes of consonants.

Letters create words and words create sentences. The eight energies exist in the world of these three: letters, words and sentences. The first five energies are the five senses of hearing, touch, seeing, taste and smell. These are followed by the three energies of mind, intellect and limited ego.

Transcendental speech is not uttered through the lips, nor though the mind or any other medium. It is soundless sound, which resides in our own universal consciousness. It is the supreme sound that has no sound. It is the life of the other three kinds of speech – namely, *pashyanti*, *madhyama* and *vaikharee.* Supreme speech is said to be centered in the heart, the location of madhyama speech, while the tongue is at the location of vaikharee speech. We shall return to this aspect of speech later in the chapter.

All sounds become manifest and are carried from the soundless centre. This is why the whole universe evolves from sound. This is the foundation of the concept of wholeness, as reflected in the power of the letters of the alphabet. We shall now extend our understanding of the inherent wholeness in the alphabet to wholeness in language itself and the prism of word meaning.

THE ILLUSORY FRAGMENTATION OF LANGUAGE

Language is innate and without a beginning. It has been in existence as long as living beings have been in existence. While it is only one of the important factors involved in thought, communication and the organisation of human society in general, it is clearly of key significance. Therefore, to enquire into the role of language structure in helping to bring about fragmentation in thought would seem to be of value at this juncture.

As a preliminary step on this path, we may ask whether any features of the commonly used language tend to sustain and propagate fragmentation, as well as to reflect it. A cursory examination shows that an important feature of this kind is the subject-verb-object structure of sentences, which is common to the grammar and syntax of modern languages. This structure implies that all action arises in a separate entity – the subject – and that, in cases described by a transitive verb, this action crosses over the space between the subject and another separate entity, the object.

If the verb is intransitive, as in *he is moved*, the action is still considered to be either a property of the subject or a reflexive action of the subject, in the sense that the words 'he is moved' may be taken to mean that he moves himself or allows himself to be moved.

This pervasive structure influences the whole of life, favouring a function of thought that tends to divide things into separate entities. These entities are then conceived of as essentially fixed and static in their nature. When this view is carried to its limit, one arrives at the prevailing scientific world view in which everything is regarded as ultimately constituted out of a set of basic particles of fixed nature.

If we consider the sentence 'It is raining', it would be more accurate to say, 'Rain is going on' or 'Rain is occurring'. As this is the actuality, would it not be possible for the syntax and grammatical form of language to be changed so as to give a basic role to the verb rather than to the noun? This alone would help to end the kind of fragmentation indicated above. For, as we know, verbs describe actions and movements, which flow into each other and merge without sharp separations or breaks.

In some ancient languages, such as Hebrew, the verb was taken as primary in the sense described above. Thus the root of almost all words in Hebrew was a certain verbal form, and adverbs, adjectives and nouns were obtained by modifying the verbal form with prefixes and suffixes, and in other ways. However, in modern Hebrew the actual usage is similar to that of English, in that the noun is given a primary role in its meaning, even though in the formal grammar everything is still built from the verb as a root.

Principles of Language

Language (wak) has four levels or phases: speech (vaikharee), mental/intellectual or potential speech (madhyama), the latent totality of units (pashyanti), and the pure, basic language principle (*para pashyanti-rupa*).

Language consists of three classes of units: phoneme (*varna*), word (*pada*) and sentence (*vakya*). The sentence, word and phoneme are unitary entities. They only appear to be made up of parts when they are being perceived (due to association with sound, which by nature has a sequence) and when conscious or subconscious grammatical analysis is being carried out. The parts, although accepted on the practical level and on the level of analysis, do not exhaust the whole, for language is infinite. For example, there is no numerical limit to the number of sentences possible in a language.

All cognitions are infused with language, and every cognition is unitary – that is, devoid of division and sequence. Cognitions merely appear to have parts or distinct elements because of the diversity of objects transferred to them. Cognition is self-manifest. The distinctions we draw between the sentence, the cogniser proceeding toward cognising, the instrument of cognition, the fact of cognition and the reflected form of the object are only conceptual; in reality, the entities spoken of are not physically distinct.

The language in the mind of the speaker is the cause of the audible language which is expressed in words and sentences. When the speaker seeks to superimpose linguistic form onto his or her intended meaning, the language appears to change its nature into something else (the meaning) and projects itself as sounds from the vocal organs. Thus, the unchanging language principle appears to be changing. It manifests through the imperceptible pervasive sounds which are articulated by the vocal organs. The journey begins from gross sound and travels to the stage of speech, which we receive through the medium of language. Thus, the meaning or the idea, although single and whole, appears to have parts which have been sequentially arranged. Just as awareness by its very nature apprehends its own form as well as that of its object, likewise in language, the forms of both the meaning and the language principle itself are illuminated. We can compare this to a visual artist who paints in stages a figure (s)he sees as a single entity.

The Use of the Spoken Word

Let us explore the different ways in which human beings use the tool of the spoken word. For communication to be effective, the person who is speaking and the person who is hearing must derive the same meaning from the sound that is organised as speech. Otherwise, the speaker will speak with an intent to communicate a particular thought but it will be received by the listener as something entirely different. So, the listener and the speaker must share a common language. The importance of this is obvious in the realm of music, where the music is a language used to communicate emotions and thoughts. The listener needs to understand the meter and the rhythm in order to experience or understand the meaning of the piece of music.

But there is more to this kind of communication if it is to be effective. The speaker and listener must share the content that is captured by a word. For example, if I ask a child to bring me an apple, it is possible that (s)he will bring a book in which an apple is drawn because (s)he has been told that 'A is for apple'.

Every word has a history and this history is custom-made, shaped by the experience of the listener. 'Let us go to Cambridge' will mean a journey to the world-renowned university city in the UK to some, and a visit to the town of the same name in California in the USA to others.

Effective communication also requires that the listener has been prepared to receive the message and to comprehend it. A reference to 'quantum mechanics' will be meaningless to someone who is not even conversant with the 'ABC' of the subject, whereas the same set of words will be enlightening and exhilarating for those who have studied the subject.

So if we seek to communicate without preparing the listener to receive and absorb the meaning of our words, the communication will go waste. The recipient or listener can be likened to a container with a certain capacity. If the capacity of the container is one litre and we pour two litres of water into it, then obviously one whole litre will overflow and be wasted. The responsibility for this wastage lies not with the container but with the person who has poured more than the container can accommodate. Therefore, an attempt to communicate beyond the listener's capacity to absorb is wasteful.

The effectiveness of communication between two human beings is also determined by how an idea is delivered. In other words, communication is conditioned by the context, which itself is defined by several factors, and within which the communication can be direct or indirect. There are three manifest forms of communication: instruction, advice and practice. When we communicate with a child, for example, we often employ the first form. If the child is about to put her hand in the fire, we scream at her to stop. Communication may take the second form, of advice, when speaking with an adult who has fallen into a bad habit, such as alcoholism. The effectiveness of this form of communication depends on the speaker's skill to communicate to the listener the harmful effects of alcoholism and the benefits of giving up this habit. Different forms of communication are required when talking to a child and to an adult; the form employed when addressing a cynic is different from the communication expressed to an empathetic person. Men and women, young and old people all require different forms of communication.

Instruction, advice, and practice or example are forms of communication in which ideas travel from one person to another and can be noted as they travel. In contrast, the subtlest form of communication is totally unobtrusive. Here the communication is almost telepathic; it is instantaneous, like a flash of light travelling at great speed, known in Sanskrit as *samvid*. Ideas can also be communicated through metaphors or allegories, in prose as well as in verse. Subtle messages are often communicated as riddles. History is preserved and retrieved as narratives, folk tales, dialogues, myths, stories, novels and epics. In science, complex principles are communicated as mathematical formulae. The same word in the same language acquires different meanings in different disciplines, conveying, for example, a different idea in history, geography or computer science.

Word as Meaning

A word is a collection of letters, but the word needs to become a whole in order to acquire a meaning. Each of the letters or syllables of a word means nothing in itself. So a word is a clear example of the fact that the whole is not merely the sum of many parts.

There is a whole constellation of meanings around words; these meanings bring forth responses from us; and these responses tie us to the world more effectively than any rope. From letters, a word is formed with its own meaning. From words, a sentence is formed with its own meaning. That meaning carries an image. Once an image is formed we begin to feel good or bad; and when either feeling arises, it is swiftly followed by the fruits of these feelings.

If we separate the letters of a particular word, the letters themselves carry no meaning. For example, let us take the word 'mother'. If we just say these letters M-O-T-H-E-R one at a time, in themselves they carry no meaning. But when we combine these letters and say the word 'mother', it has its own power, its own meaning and it bears fruit too. The fruit of words is either painful or pleasurable; sometimes it is sweet, sometimes bitter, sometimes sour.

According to Kashmiri Shaivism, speech contains within herself the whole collection of powers of the sounds of the alphabet, and brings the sphere of the empirical subject into being through successive stages of the manifestation of sound. This exploration of the power of the letters of the alphabet (*matrika-shakti*) is one of the most fascinating aspects of Shaivism, which acknowledges fifty letters and asserts that the power has taken on the forms of fifty supraphysical energies that exist in these fifty letters – as we noted earlier in this chapter. By assuming the form of these letters, the power deceives everyone.

Yet those individuals who understand the power of the letters can use this understanding to attain liberation. To comprehend the full power of matrika, we must begin once again at the beginning, with the creation of the universe, exploring the process of creation from an ontological perspective – that is, how each of the tattwas is the basis for a specific state of being. We can then proceed to look at how creation manifests vibrationally through the power of sound, known as 'supreme speech'.

Each of the fifty phonemes of the Sanskrit alphabet symbolises an extremely subtle vibratory level and is a power (shakti) in itself, as noted above. Taken together, these vibrations create, support and transform the universe. According to the traditions of Sanskrit grammar, the fifty forms of power are arranged in an order and divided into eight groups, each of which is known as a varga. Every one of these powers is a matrika, a term translated as 'mother' because out of the womb of this 'mother' springs the created universe.

In speech, communication is always through complete utterances. The speaker thinks and the listener understands the utterance as a single unit, unless the person listening is unfamiliar with the language being spoken. But anyone who knows the language well will comprehend the verbal expression as a whole, grasping the meaning in an instantaneous flash of insight (*pratibha*).

The fact that the expression has to be through the medium of phonemes and through a temporal or spatial series does not warrant the conclusion that it is made up of parts. The sphota theory asserts that hearing the whole sentence is the real experience, while the apparent experience of hearing the sound particles is only for those who do not know the language being spoken.[5]

This entire process, in fact, is a single whole. Sphota arises in the mind and takes shape in the intellect. As mentioned earlier, knowledge is captured in words which are manifestations of sound in various forms. When we use the word for the first time, the pictures it seeks to convey leave a very feeble trace on our intellect. Repetition of that word deepens the picture etched in our mind, and as the picture deepens, the word begins to acquire that meaning. In other words, when we hear a word for the first time, the meaning is a little feeble. When we hear it for the second time, it becomes clearer and, over the course of time, the relationship between a specific word and the meaning it conveys becomes entrenched and inseparable. It is at that stage that we unfortunately begin to regard word and its meaning as separate entities, and fragmentation occurs. Although it is generally believed that it is the word which is the cause of the meaning, the fact is that the two are intertwined. The relationship between this sphota and the meaning that it communicates is like the relationship between gold and an ornament made of that gold.

Sphota has neither a beginning nor an end. It is not organised in a sequence, nor is it otherwise. The relationship between sphota and sound is that between a reflection and the object which is reflected. Knowledge manifests itself but also illuminates the object of knowledge. Similarly, sphota manifests the word and also illuminates the object of the content contained within the word. When an artist paints a picture on a canvas, that picture is already present in his mind before he draws it on the canvas. Similarly, sphota is already present in the mind before it flashes like a light through the medium of sound. Generally speaking, the word is considered primary and the content secondary. However, it is clear that as long as the uttered word is not able to communicate the meaning it is unable to illuminate the existence of the object it seeks to communicate or convey. Therefore, it is of utmost importance to remember the intertwined and inseparable relationship between the word and its meaning, and thereby to experience wholeness through the prism of word and meaning.

EDITOR'S NOTE:

To further their study of this subject, we encourage readers to refer to Section Six of RK Mishra's first volume, Before the Beginning and After the End. This section contains Chapter Seventeen, 'Word and Meaning: The Importance of Grammar in the Study of the Vedas', and Chapter Eighteen, 'Language and the Seer-scientists of the Vedas'. Readers are also recommended to refer to the sections of RK Mishra's other volumes that are indicated in the Endnotes to this chapter.

Chapter 20

THE PRINCIPLE AND APPLICATION OF VARNA

Varna, as an important principle of social organisation in Bharatavarsha, has been a subject of furious controversy, especially during the past 300 years. Much of this controversy has arisen from the translation of 'varna' as 'one of the four traditional social classes of Hindu India',[6] notwithstanding the fact that the literal meaning of the word varna is 'colour'. Stretching their imagination to (mis)interpret Sanskrit words to fit Western mental and sociological constructs, European scholars have speculated that varna signifies that 'class distinctions were originally based on differences in degree of skin pigmentation'. All this tendentious 'speculation' is to sustain the theory of pitting the 'fairer-skinned Aryans' against the 'darker aboriginals'. The ridiculousness of the assertion that colours were frequently used as classifiers becomes evident from the reference that the *Yajur Veda* is divided into two groups of texts – 'white' and 'black'. Clearly these commentators have not taken the time to refer to the use of *shukla* (white) and *krishna* (black) in the Gita.[7]

The varnas have been known since the late *Rig Veda* hymn 10:90, in which it is declared that the *brahmana* (priest), the *kshatriya* (nobleman), the *vaishya* (commoner) and the *shoodra* (serf) issued forth at creation from the mouth, arms, thighs and feet of the primeval person (*purusha*). In the ancient description, far greater emphasis is placed on the functions of the classes than on hereditary membership – in contradistinction to caste, which emphasises heredity over function.

Smoothly, but without any rational justification, varna is described as class, as in the statement that 'the system of the four classes (*caturvarnya*) is fundamental to the views the traditional lawgivers held of society.' Then comes the attempt to equate varna with *jat*, 'also spelled jat, caste, in Hindu society. The term is derived from the Sanskrit *jata,* "born" or "brought into existence," and indicates a form of existence determined by birth.'

However, this assertion has to face the fact that although the lawgivers of the traditional Hindu codes (*Dharma-shastra*) themselves tend to treat *jatis* as varnas (social classes) and try to account on other occasions for jatis as products of alliances between the four varnas (brahmanas, kshatriyas, vaishyas, and shoodras) and their descendants; a sharp distinction should be made between jati as a limited regional endogamous group of families, and varna as a universal all-Indian model of social class. The official Hindu view gives second place to jati as an aberration of varna. This has also to contend with the reality of the multitudinousness of castes, explained as being the result of hypergamous and hypogamous alliances between the four classes and their descendants.

Use of the term 'caste' to characterise social organisation dates to the middle of the sixteenth century. *Casta* (from

Latin *castus*, 'chaste') in the sense of purity of breed was employed by the Portuguese to describe the division of society in Bharatavarsha into socially ranked occupational categories. Subsequently cast, or caste, became established in English and major European languages (notably Dutch and French) in the same specific sense.

The highly misleading translation of varna as caste is found not only in sociological literature but also in translations of and commentaries to Bhagavadgita and other related literature.[8] The varna system, thus distorted and misinterpreted, has been the target of massive assault. Even some 'modern' reformers, who otherwise laud the Vedas, have denounced it. An entire generation of neo-literates, overawed by western interpretation of Vedic terminology, denounces the four varnas as the root of social divisiveness and, therefore, of the weak and fragmented social fabric of India. Some devotees of the Vedas have ascribed this 'harmful' tendency to the Age of the Puranas. According to these critics, pure Vedic literature prescribes common 'dharma' for everyone; the 'degeneration' only set in during the Puranic Age. Perturbed by the disunity and fragmentation in their society, they believe that one 'dharma' for all can unite the people and encourage them to flow in a single stream. This, they believe, would lead to the prosperity of the nation, the well-being of society and the resurgence of Bharatavarsha. They assert that the division of people between brahmana, kshatriya, vaishya and shoodra – and consequently between higher and lower castes – is a human invention. In reality, they argue, all men (and women) are equal; in the eyes of god, no one is 'higher' or 'lower' than another. Therefore, all should follow the same norms and rules of society and be equal in all aspects of daily life. They maintain that the Vedas direct a social system bereft of any discrimination, which enjoins everyone to follow the same dharma. In support of this view, they cite several Veda mantras and verses from the Gita.[9]

This entire argument flows from a colossal ignorance of the principles that prevail in the cosmic order. The self-denigration is a product of the distortion of theoretical constructs underlying the concepts of social engineering based on the Vedic sciences. To deal with this situation, it is necessary to study the conceptual framework around the maxim that distances individuals from one another, and discriminates between these individuals operating in the cosmic domain. It also requires a deeper understanding of the meaning of dharma – which is not religion – and an ability to discern the principles of varna.

Animated controversy has also raged as to whether the categorisation of individuals according to varna is based on birth or on attributes, vocation or individual functions. This debate is, however, rendered meaningless when it is fully understood that varna is not a phenomenon specific to human beings, but also pervades the entire cosmic order and applies equally to individuals outside the human domain. Once this is fully comprehended, the meaning of the verse in the Gita which states, 'I have created four varnas by dividing (individuals) according to qualities and functions,' acquires a totally different dimension. This in turn will transform our understanding of the proposition that every sentient and insentient individual in the cosmos is subjected to varna, and the implications and applications of this to human society.

Since the controversy over varna continues to rage, it is worth spending a little time on looking at various theories and arguments. Broadly speaking, the attitude to varna can be grouped into four categories. The 'orthodox' section upholds that the varna system is not a human invention but has been existent since time immemorial. 'God', who created this universe, is the originator of the varna system. Brahmana varna emerged from the mouth of that *virat purusha*, kshatriya varna emerged from the arms, vaishya varna from the stomach and shoodra varna from the feet. Since the varna system is divine, it is based on birth.

Another school of devotees of Veda upholds the view that the varna system is endorsed by the Vedas. According to this viewpoint, the system is based on the qualities, attributes, functions and vocation of an individual. In the Vedic age, the inclusion of a person in a particular varna depended on that person's vocation or principal attributes. This school dismisses references in the *Shastras* to varna being based on birth as subsequent interpolations by selfish brahmanas in order to ensure their own supremacy. Proponents of this view assert that as long as the varna system was based on qualities and functions, the country continued to prosper. Its decline dates to the time when the varna system came to be considered as being based on birth. Therefore, they advocate that it is the duty of a genuine devotee of the Vedas to reject this dictum of the Puranic Age and accept the principle that the varna system is based on an individual's attributes and vocation.

The reformers proclaim that the varna system did not exist when Bharatavarsha was at the pinnacle of its glory – that is, during the Vedic Age. At that time there was no conflict among the various varnas nor any tension between high and low. There was no question of touchability or untouchability. All human beings belonged to one and the same 'category' and enjoyed equal rights in all activities. They all worshipped together, and social intercourse was simple and non-discriminatory. The pursuit of truth, non-violence, refraining from stealing and so forth formed the principal dharma of that Age. But, they assert, unfortunately the human intellect became perverted, the moral fibre weakened and social disarray set in. It was during the Puranic Age, they claim, that shortsightedness gave birth to the evils of the varna system which is at the root of caste divisions and caste jealousies. This has had the effect of weakening India's unity and moral structure. The imposition of caste discrimination and varna divisions on society enfeebled the nation and fragmented the society, as the poisonous seeds of 'high' and 'low' were sown. Those who claimed to belong to the 'higher' varna heaped untold atrocities on the 'lower' varnas and the 'outcastes'. They invented rules, rituals and religious texts through which to perpetrate their domination and validate their oppression. The reformers assert that these same religious texts which endorse and support the varna as a form of caste oppression should make us hang our heads in shame. All those who wish to promote their country's welfare should do all in their power to eradicate the menace of the varna system. Only then will our country be able to progress.

In the fourth category, fall 'neutral' critics who reject the claim that there was no varna system in the Vedic Age. They assert that a study of social and civic policies of that Age leads us to the conclusion that the varna system prevailed at that time to maintain order in society. It can definitely be said that at that time the varna system was primarily based on functions and had nothing to do with caste or birth. A person was included in a varna depending on what (s)he was doing. Subsequently, it was felt that it would not be possible to organise society on a stable basis as long as the varna system remained linked to vocation. As a result, the notion of the varna system being based on birth came into vogue, so that what was originally based on vocation and function came to be based on birth.

It is difficult to argue with scholars belonging to the third category, because they draw support from religious texts when it suits them and dismiss those portions of the texts as 'interpolations' when it does not suit them. In the Vedic tradition, the Vedas are regarded as 'proof' of the validity of a proposition. But those who are selective should be treated as being equal to those who do not accept the authority of the Vedas at all. This leaves those who accept that the varna system is validated by the Vedas but differ on whether it is based on birth or on an individual's vocation and attributes. Numerous arguments have been put forward to support both.

Varna in the Cosmic Order

The word 'varna' evolves from a root signifying sustainability as well as motivation or stimulation.[10] The term embraces both interpretations, indicating that varna creates, sustains and motivates.

Atman or Brahma, the source and the origin of all creations, has three facets. The visible universe, made of the five basic gross material elements, is the facet which is 'created' from that source. It envelops the spontaneous expansion of consciousness, which is the true nature of Brahma or atma. At the heart of this universe resides the regulatory factor that is the incidental cause of this bewildering diversity, and this is known as *antaryami*. The third facet is the all-pervasive factor, which permeates within and outside the boundaries of the universe and is neither a cause nor a consequence. It remains unattached and is only a support. Thus, the atma of the universe is discernible in these three facets and has been described as *parabrahma*.

These three facets are related to the *awyaya*, *akshara* and *kshara* dimensions of cosmic totality. The kshara dimension of atma is the material cause of the universe; akshara is the regulator; and awyaya is the unattached, uninvolved factor. Of these three, awyaya is predominantly imbued with the brilliance of consciousness, akshara is imbued with the power of action, and kshara is imbued with the force of matter. It is this third factor – namely, matter – which embraces the light of consciousness and the power of motion to stimulate the creative process. This dimension envelops the light of consciousness.[11]

This state of kshara when it wraps or envelops consciousness is called 'varna'. It is divided into four, and the four 'varnas' come into being. Parabrahma is kshara in its created state. Varna or consonant in its created state is *shabda Brahma*. In the former (parabrahma), only the material portion (kshara) is visible and the akshara portions remain concealed (*awyakta*); whereas in the domain of shabda Brahma, sphota and *swara* remain unmanifest.

This universe is divided into 'shabda' (word) and 'artha' (meaning). But 'meaning' here does not stand for a verbal explanation. Rather, it signifies the 'substance' or the 'material entity' represented in the word. For example, 'horse' is a word, and the meaning of horse is the four-legged animal that we ride. Artha is the substance signified by word. Both of these are related to varna.[12] The universe comprises entities which have a name and a form. The name signifies word or shabda, and the form is indicated by the content that the word depicts. In that sense, the universe is an entity which is permeated with varna. The universe – an aggregation of word and meaning – remains on track as long as the varna system remains in order. Language loses its coherence when varna or vowels are thrown into disarray. Similarly, when the varna system is thrown into disarray, the material universe is subject to chaos and disorder. Varna sustains matter and fortifies its existence. The boundaries set out by varna are called *chhanda* (meter).

An exhaustive study of the science of phonetics based on the Vedic sciences helps in comprehending the mutuality and intertwined nature of parabrahma, the source of all cosmic creations, and shabda brahma, the words that define, discern and capture the innumerable individuals comprising the universe. It also helps us to understand the nature of varna, both in words and in the universe captured by those words. A student must understand the difference between akshara and varna. Akshara is not 'letter' (as postulated by some western linguists). Letter is a means of writing and not a category of sound. Unlike other languages, there is no correlation between what is written and what is read in Sanskrit, for in this language there is an inexorable relationship between the two. The Vedic scientists have categorised 'akshara' and 'varna' distinctly and separately.

The varnas are closer to phoneme, and akshara is the original sound.

Shrimad Bhagwad Purana is held in special esteem among all the Puranas. Those who uphold that the varna system is based on birth are disappointed even by Shrimad Bhagwad Purana.[13] The *Kalpasutras* lay down the norms of application of the principles of the Vedic sciences, and very clearly opine that, by birth, everyone is a shoodra. Only through individual 'refinement' and study, hard work, performance of *yajnya* and other practices does one become a brahmana.[14] As the rituals of refinement give rise to the traits of a *dwija* – 'twice-born' – one who has not gone through the second-thread ceremony is called *vratya*. The 'refined' dwija is forbidden to have meals and so forth with a vratya. The many prohibitions and restrictions imposed on brahmanas also underline the crucial importance of actions, behaviour and functions. The fact that several *Smritis* speak of people becoming 'degenerate' from the jatis if they are guilty of some undesirable actions lends strength to this view.[15]

By engaging in conduct befitting and appropriate to a brahmana, a shoodra can become a brahmana. Likewise, by engaging in actions and behaviour appropriate to a shoodra, a brahmana can become a shoodra, according to the Vedic text *Gopatha Brahmana*. Just as an elephant made of wood is elephant in name only, similarly an illiterate and uneducated brahmana is brahmana only in name. Brahmanas who ignore the study of the Vedas enjoined for them, instead remaining preoccupied in other activities, become shoodras along with their family members within their lifetime. And brahmanas who do not perform *agnihotra* become ineffective as a brahmana, and the blessings of such a person are of no value.[16]

Metaphors for Transformation

Aitereya Brahmana records a narrative which beautifully illustrates this point: once upon a time the *rishis* or seer-scientists were beginning an important yajnya ceremony – *satra yajnya* – lasting for 100 days on the banks of the river Saraswati when Kavasha, the son of Elusha, joined the gathering with a view to participating. But the *rishis* objected: how could this illegitimate child, who was a gambler and a non-brahmana, join in the yajnya? After consulting among themselves they threw him out of the precincts of the yajnya, dragged him over a long distance and left him in an isolated place with no water and nothing but burning sand. This was the punishment meted out to him for daring to think that he could engage in actions for which only a brahmana is eligible.

Kavasha was in extreme distress from hunger and thirst in that hot, isolated and hazardous place. He recalled the *Aaponoptiya Sutra* of the Vedas and began to recite it aloud. As he did so, a stream of cold water sprang up nearby and rapidly spread in the Saraswati region, up to the place where the *rishis* were performing yajnya. They were very surprised to see this unexpected stream of water, and then they realised that it was due to Kavasha having harnessed the supraphysical energies (*devatas*). They went to the place where they had left him and found the source of the stream there. Recognising his qualities, they paid him due honour and respect and began to practise the *Aaponoptiya Sutra*.[17]

Thus, Kavasha, although a non-brahmana, found a place of honour in *Rig Veda* as the seer-scientist who 'saw' (discovered) the *Aaponoptiya Sutra*.[18] This episode has lent strength to the view that, while some orthodox people seek to prevent shoodras from studying the Vedas, a non-brahmana, shoodra can occupy a venerable place in the annals of the seer-scientists.

Similarly, the story of Vishwamitra is well-known and is endorsed by Manu.[19] Initially a kshatriya known for his unbridled and violent behaviour, Vishwamitra later engaged in actions by which he became a brahmarshi (a brahmana seer-scientist) from a kshatriya seer-scientist. The stories of Vitihotra, Rishabhaputra and others are also relevant and instructive in this connection. In fact, Bhagavadgita speaks of the transformation of a whole family because of the impact of a change in their actions.[20]

The *Harivansha Purana* endorses the fact that the varna system is based on actions and is determined by the conduct of a person.[21] To support their contention, several orthodox scholars draw upon some Veda mantras which state that brahmanas were born from Brahma's mouth.[22] It would be reasonable to assert that such a statement merely emphasises the fact that a brahmana has the same place of honour in society as the mouth does in the body. This superiority is based on the individual brahmana's knowledge and erudition. Similarly, kshatriyas, who represent the physical strength of society, are like the arms of a person. These are metaphors, which it would be ridiculous to take literally. Who would assert that a brahmana is literally born from the mouth?

The Veda mantras describe *parmeshwara* as being 'without a body'.[23] Where he is portrayed as having limbs, the mantra describes him as having hands and feet on all sides.[24] These mantras communicate some conceptual constructs; it would be erroneous to literally draw the conclusion that various varnas are actually produced from different parts of Brahma's body.

Some *Brahmana Shrutis* state that brahmanas are born from *gayatri* meter.[25] We need to understand what such statements imply, for obviously brahmanas are not physically born from a meter of eight letters. Such statements must be understood in context. Gayatri is that mantra to which brahmanas dedicate themselves. All references in *Shrutis* and *Smritis* to the term 'born', 'produced' and so forth are used in the context of the varnas, so the meaning should be related to the context and viewed as a figure of speech, rather than being taken literally. All this leads to the conclusion that the varna system is based on conduct, work and vocation and not on birth.

There are four principal sources of power in a social structure: knowledge, government, wealth, and physical strength. While those endowed with physical strength are certainly powerful, those vested with the power of wealth are able to influence and dominate them. Yet in all societies the power of wealth is subordinated to those who run the administration and government. In the final analysis, then, all sources of power are regulated by the power of knowledge.

The varna system reflects this social reality. There is a tendency to compare these with the western classification of society into clergy, military, merchants and labourers. Based on that comparison, the brahmanas, kshatriyas, vaishyas and shoodras are categorised in a hierarchical manner. But any similarity between the two social schemes is superficial, because it must not be forgotten that the varna system, used as a basis for social engineering by the Vedic scientists, is founded on an understanding of the interrelationship of the supraphysical forces operating in nature. A varna is not specific to society and its members. Rather, it extends to all individuals and species in the scheme of nature. In that sense it is not arbitrary, but derives its logic from nature's own organisation. All four varnas must remain aligned to ensure harmony and tranquillity.

The three sources of creative vitality or *veerya* – that is, brahmana, kshatriya and vaishya – are related to the three meters of gayatri, *trishtup* and *jagati*. Gayatri permeates at dawn; *savita* prevails at noon – this is trishtup; and jagati dominates in the evening, which is *saraswati*. The direct luminosity of the sun, as well as all luminous rays radiating from the mass of every individual, is savita. The supraphysical energy radiating from savita is *savitri*. All emanating light, whether from the sun or moon or a lamp or a torch, is covered in the category of savita.

The luminosity emanating from an individual is savitri, and when reflected back it becomes gayatri. *Rig Veda* speaks of the luminous rays of the sun.[26] The rays emanating from the sun are savita, and that which is reflected back to the sun is gayatri. The supraphysical energy of agni is endowed with gayatri at dawn, and hence the earth (*prithwi*) is often called gayatri.[27]

The reflected solar luminous rays are called saraswati in the evening. *Saraswan* is the ocean of the supraphysical energy of *parameshthi*. Agni reigns during the day and soma rules at night. Since soma is related to parmeshthi, the term saraswan is used. The wak component of the saraswan ocean is called saraswati, and this is why the reflection of solar luminosity in the evening is also called saraswati.

Brahma, kshara, *vid* and shoodra are the four states of supraphysical energy predominant in four parts of the day. Gayatri is dominant in the morning. Gayatri is the supraphysical energy of agni, which is tranquil when reflected. In the process of reflection, its sharpness is calmed. This is Brahma, and it is the point of origination of the others. The luminosity dominant at noon (*savita tej*) is sharp and strong. This is kshara, which dominates when the supraphysical energy is in full bloom. In the afternoon, when the energy begins to fade, *saraswat tej* is on the decline and at this stage it is vid. The energy in the night is permeated with *tamas* characteristics, and this is shoodra. In a deeper sense, the sun is the source of every individual's atma.[28] It is the same solar *teja* (luminosity) that assumes the four forms of gayatri, savita, saraswat and tamas.

Agni related to the earth is the first supraphysical energy. The moon (*chandrama*) presides over interspace, while the sun (*soorya*) is the ruler of the solar system. In the context of the earth, moon and sun, savitri is classified into three categories. As the soma of kshatriya emanates from savitri, there are only three dynasties of kshatriya. These are descendants of agni (*agni vamsha*), descendants of the moon (chandrama), and descendants of the sun (*soorya vamsha*).

The distribution of the rights and responsibilities of the four varnas found in the social engineering system based on the Vedic sciences ensures that no single section is able to 'misuse' the powers vested in it. In a very broad sense, there is a separation of powers among the four groups.

For example, brahmanas are given the highest position in society, based on their devotion to the pursuit of knowledge and their place in society as its repository. However, the Vedic scientists were conscious of the fact that a person or group tends to become proud and arrogant on reaching the highest rung of the social ladder, and such a sense of pride could undermine the knowledge vested in brahmanas. Accordingly, the Vedic sciences restrain brahmanas from acquiring the power of wealth, or acquiring the power that comes from running a government or administration. Brahmanas are neither permitted to accumulate wealth nor to possess weapons. They are enjoined to despise the concept of 'honour'; in fact, Manu enjoins the brahmanas to treat 'honour' like poison and keep away from it.[29] Rather, they should be content with whatever they have, and satisfied with whatever becomes available to eke out a living.

Kshatriyas are endowed with the power to rule. But it was recognised by the Vedic seer-scientists that society can suffer from the grave excesses of those who possess both the power to rule and the power of wealth. When a ruler misuses the power to rule, she or he along with his or her kith and kin, is visited by total destruction.[30] Vaishyas are directed not only to take but also to give.[31] This varna is enjoined to apply wealth so as to create more wealth for the welfare of the people. Thus, every varna has 'power' coupled with duty and responsibility.

The varna system is no arbitrary arrangement. It is based on the science of the relationship between physical and supraphysical forces in the universe. It flows from the premise that the enduring well-being of human society is contingent on harmony between human behaviour and the enduring rules which govern the 'behaviour' of various individuals in the natural order. Capricious and arbitrary behaviour, which violates this spirit of harmony in discernible nature carries with it the seeds of its own destruction. Perceptive observers have wondered at the fact that the civilisation of Bharatavarsha has not perished, while the great Roman and Greek empires have disappeared without a trace. This is because our civilisation derives (or has derived so far) its inspiration from the harmonious interrelationships between the interactions of diverse and numerous individuals in the natural order.

Swayambhoo Brahma – the founder of dharma based on the principles enunciated by the seer-scientists – created a society based on these principles. They ensure harmony in human society by laying down norms of conduct that are in tune with the behaviour of numerous individuals operating in the cosmic order. This harmony is reflected from time immemorial in the relationships between sun and moon, sun, moon and earth, light and water, and many other individuals.

The Role of Agni

We act in three ways: by thought, by speech, and by physical effort. These three constitute mental behaviour, verbal behaviour and behaviour in which we apply our physical energy. Mental action consists of desires; verbal action consists of words; and physical energy or action consists of effort. The strength of the body is the source of all these forms of action, and our body derives its strength from the supraphysical energy of agni. This important supraphysical energy dwells in our body and is discernible in the five gross material elements (*panchamahabhootas*). The greater the vision of agni in an individual, the healthier and stronger that individual's physical body will be. This strength propels and regulates the above-mentioned three forms of action, and thus agni is the source of all forms of physical action. A deeper analysis leads to the conclusion that all action – not only in the physical order but also in the material and supraphysical orders and in yajnya (the interface and interaction of various supraphysical energies) – flows from the fundamental tattwa of agni. This agni assumes four forms in accordance with its applications.[32]

The performer of yajnya, known as the *yajaman*, has to blend these four forms of agni in order to achieve the objectives of yajnya. All four forms of agni are permeated with mana, prana and wak. The seer-scientists tell us unequivocally that agni is permeated with wak.[33] Wherever agni is present, prana and mana are also there. In the course of yajnya, a harmonious relationship needs to be established between these four forms of agni and the mana, prana, wak components with the mana, prana and wak of the yajaman. This huge project cannot be executed by the yajaman alone, and so help must be commissioned in the form of four *ritwiks*, described in the four technical terms of Brahma, *adhwaryu*, *hota* and *udgata*. The ritwiks assist the yajaman in establishing a harmonious relationship with the different components of mana, prana and wak, and the four forms of agni are the co-ordinators of the whole exercise. The former three achieve this by relying on the mantras of *Rig Veda*, *Yajur Veda* and *Sama Veda*. Thus, while four people are performing actions, there is co-ordination among them and the benefit flows to the yajaman.

The same principle informs the social engineering envisaged by Manu. According to this perspective, society is perceived as one 'person' or one 'individual' who has four parts: mouth, arms, stomach and feet. All these parts are of equal importance and there is no hierarchical relationship among them. The relationship between them is functional, and any difference lies not in terms of one being 'higher' or 'lower' than the other. To put it another way, the four varnas in society – based on the principles of harmony – are complementary, and the differences are merely functional. This system does not favour one varna over another, but seeks to ensure the well-being of the whole society,

Varna as Wak

As noted earlier in this chapter, the basis of this varna system is the varna order discernible in nature. To examine this comprehensively and in detail is beyond the scope of this work. However, we shall look in some depth at varna as a component of speech (wak), to illustrate the true meaning and extent of varna. According to the principles of darshana, the relationship between words and meaning is enduring and has been so since their inception.[34] For example, when we call an object a 'pot' it would be erroneous to think that first a pot is created (that is, the object) and then the word ('pot') followed. In reality, they are co-terminous. The meaning is the content, and the word (noun) defines it. Both word and meaning originate from wak. The original *wak tattwa* is divided into two facets, *ambhrini* and saraswati, and these are the source of the content (meaning) and the words (shabda). Parabrahma, discernible in the content which constitutes the cosmos, evolves from the ambhrini aspect of wak while shabda brahma evolves from the saraswati aspect of wak. This is why all the structural components of parabrahma are discernible in the structural components of the universe.

Now let us look at the domain of words or shabda Brahma. Wak is the origin of the universe. It comprises the order of content (meaning) and the order of words which define and describe that content. Prajapati or atma comprises mana, prana and wak, and these are three developed forms of prana – a generic term for supraphysical energy. The same prana evolves into three forms in the process of creation, and this basic 'causative' factor is known as '*rishi*'. *Pitara* evolves from this original supraphysical energy, and the asura, *gandharva* and *deva pranas* evolve from that. The entire sentient and insentient universe is created by the interaction and interface of these deva and asura supraphysical energies.

In the course of its transformation from supraphysical energy to speech, prana passes through seven states. In the context of the physical order, these states are fire (*taijas)*, energy (prana*)*, wind (vayu), breath (*shwasa*), sound (nada), word (*shruti)* and letter/syllable (varna). A brief reference to these seven states will be helpful in taking this concept further.

A basic current of energy flows along the human spine from its base to the suture in the centre of the head, which is often referred to as *Brahma granthi* or *trinosthi prana*. The body remains erect because this current of energy keeps the spine firm and strong. But this prana becomes subdued with advancing age, causing many human beings to require some support, such as a stick, to walk and stand erect. While this prana remains in its location in its original form, it is called *taijas prana*.

When a desire arises in the mind, it spurs the individual on to expend effort. All effort is based on the agni in the body. Therefore, desire stimulates this agni in the first instance. Once provoked, agni is full of power and vigour, as is trinosthi prana (teja). Stimulated by agni, trinosthi prana begins to circulate upwards in the body. In this state, taijas prana is known as vayu (wind).

This process does not conclude until the desire is satisfied by achieving the goal. The more this process continues, the more stimulated and provoked the agni in the body becomes, which in turn has an effect on the 'wind' circulating in the body. As the action-reaction on vayu or wind intensifies, a stage comes when the wind circulating in the body is subdued. At that time, the subdued state of prana is called breath (shwasa), and the wind makes a subtle sound.

This breath then travels to the 'core' that is the head. Just as words emanating from the mouth resound and resonate when they hit the walls of a cave or some other kind of obstruction, similarly, the air which is now in the state called 'breath' circulates in the 'space' of the 'cave' of the head, hits the walls and is transformed into a sound, known as 'nada'. This sound permeates the 'cave' and spreads out, in much the same way as the roar of a lion permeates the space around the animal. This state of sound is called 'shruti', and ultimately becomes the basis of vowels and syllables. When, for example, a singer murmurs something before articulating his or her song, this 'internal prattle' is shruti. When this shruti state finally spreads out externally, this becomes the sixth state and is known as *swar*. (Musicians call it *alap*.) Swar clashes with the chest, throat and heart, and this clash of sound gives rise to the varnas. This is the seventh state of energy, which began as taijas prana, and these seven states of prana are clearly enunciated by the seer-scientists in the Vedas.[35] The theory of the seven pranas transforming into seven states of sound (*prana saptak vijnan*) as enunciated in *Rig Mantra* is spelled out by Panini in the theories of *shiksha*.[36]

Because the supraphysical energy of prana is formless, it is incapable of any operation without the support of an individual which has a form. By embracing wak, which has a form, the formless supraphysical energy acquires the above-noted seven states. These seven states can also be described as seven facets of speech, and as seven dimensions of the supraphysical energy that causes speech. Of these seven states, we shall now focus on three – prana, swara and varna – in the context of this study of the varna system.

The application of speech is divided into four forms: varna, akshara, pada and vakya. Varna is defined as a letter or a syllable; the aggregation of varna forms akshara; and pada is defined as a part, portion, division, portion of a verse, quarter, line of a stanza. It is also a word or an injected word or the stem of a noun in the middle case.[37] Vakya is defined as a sentence or a statement.[38] Sequentially, the succeeding structures are constituted from the preceding forms, so that akshara is constituted of varna, pada is constituted of akshara, and vakya is constituted of pada.

Just as the aggregation of varna forms akshara, the aggregation of akshara makes pada; and a sentence comprises an aggregation of pada. In some cases, a single varna is also regarded as akshara. a (v), i (b) and u (m) are regarded as varnas, as is akshara related to swara and varna. Some aksharas are also treated as padas. ch (p), wa (o), ha (°), hi (°h) and na (u) are regarded as aksharas as well as pada. Some padas are regarded as a sentence, but these should be treated as exceptions, which only validate the rule enunciated earlier.

Varna is a tattwa – a basic unit – and is divided into two: vowels (swara) and consonants (*vyanjana*). The two combine in akshara.[39] In fact, this is how varna and akshara are differentiated. Sphota, a third tattwa, differs from both vowels and consonants. Sphota represents awyaya manifested as mana. Swara represents akshara manifested as prana. And varna represents kshara manifested as wak. Parabrahma has three aspects – awyaya, akshara and kshara – while shabda brahma's three aspects are sphota, swara and varna. The two sets correspond to each other.

Awyaya manifests in the form of mana, and is dominated by consciousness or knowledge (*jnana*). Akshara manifests in the form of prana, and is dominated by activity. Kshara manifests as wak, and is dominated by 'substance'. The wak tattwa, in which are incorporated the mana and prana components, is the point of departure of parabrahma which incorporates awyaya, akshara and kshara. The *sama wak* causes the evolution of shabda brahma, which is an aggregation of sphota, swara and varna. Because both parabrahma and shabda brahma are aspects of wak – a basic factor in the cosmic reality – there is an interwoven identity of word and meaning.

Awyaya is an enduring phenomenon (amrita), and so is sphota. Akshara is enduring on its own but becomes a changeable entity when it incorporates kshara within its embrace. Similarly, vowels are enduring and unchanging but become changeable in association with consonants. Kshara is changing and perishable (*mrityu pradhan*). Varna is likewise. Awyaya is the support and base of akshara and kshara, and sphota is too. The domain of kshara cannot survive without the support of akshara. Similarly, consonants cannot survive without the support of vowels.

The infinite and seamless awyaya becomes akshara when it acquires a centre. So the enduring and changing aspects of akshara – a fusion of *rasa* and *bala* – become kshara in its perishable, changing aspects. Thus, it is awyaya which, in successive states, is transformed into akshara and kshara and thenceforth assumes the form of every individual in this universe. In the role of kshara as the spur of creation, awyaya can be described as the 'creator' of the word of 'varna'. Yet in its pure state, awyaya is perceived as being uninvolved in creation. This duality is explained in Bhagavadgita,[40] wherein it is stated that awyaya has 'produced' or 'created' four varnas in accordance with a quality (*guna*) and functions (karma).

Varna in the Supraphysical Order

To briefly recap on earlier explanations, existence pervades all individuals and comprises mana, prana and wak. Of these three, wak has two classifications: enduring and transitory. Wind or vayu emanates from the latter and produces fire (agni). Water is the dense state of agni, and earth (prithvi) is the dense state of water. Prana is subtler than wak and mana is subtler than prana. Energy is subtler than matter and mind is subtler than energy.[41] The five gross material elements are grosser states of wak, whereas mana and prana are very subtle entities. The aggregation of these elements is known as 'atma', from which the wak, or soma-related supraphysical energy permeated with prana, is produced. All material entities then follow. This is the sequence of creation.[42]

Existence is a fusion of Brahma and karma. In other words, all that exists is a product of Brahma and karma, of knowledge and action. No creation is possible by the mind (knowledge) alone. First, the will to act is generated. All actions are transient. Substance (artha) is produced in its supraphysical state, which gives rise to *pashu* and the latter creates dharma.

A succession of supraphysical energies are produced from Brahma. The first category of prana emanating from Brahma is called *kshatra*, which exists in different types with their corresponding distinctive names: *Indra*, *varun*, *soma*, *rudra*, *parjanya* and *ishan*. These devatas are permeated with the power of action. Another category of prana, called *vit*, is also produced from Brahma. This category of supraphysical energies includes vasu, rudra, aditya, *vishwadeva* and *marut*. The third category of supraphysical energies nurtures and nourishes the earth, and is called *poosha*. The fourth category of supraphysical energy nourishes the earlier three categories, and is called Brahma. All these categories of supraphysical energies need to be kept within their respective parameters. To do so is known as 'dharma', which is articulated as a principle in the Vedic texts.[43]

Indra and the devatas belonging to the category of the cosmic order are kshara. Agni is brahmana. Vasu and rudra are vaishya, and poosha is shoodra. Gayatri is the meter of agni, while jagati is the meter of vishwadeva, and poosha is free of any confines of meter. All three vital energies – Brahma, kshatra and vit – are subject to regulation, but poosha is free of all regulations. Thus, all the four varnas of brahmana, kshatriya, vaishya and shoodra are present in the 'body' of *Ishwara*.

All sentient and insentient objects in the universe are produced by these four varnas, and all four supraphysical energies exist in all individuals. Those in whom Brahma veerya is dominant are called brahmanas. The kshatra supraphysical energy predominates in kshatriya. Similarly, the supraphysical energies belonging to the vit category dominate in vaishya. And poosha is predominant in shoodra.

The atma of brahmana is made by agni. As agni has eight components, the quality of brahmana fully develops in eight years, so brahmanas become eligible to perform a yajnya after attaining that age. In harmony with this 'natural' factor, the sacred-thread ceremony is performed when children reach eight years of age. From that age onwards, they are required to follow rules and norms earmarked for brahmanas.

Indra has eleven components. Therefore, the sacred-thread ceremony of kshatriyas is performed when they attain the age of eleven. The *jagati* meter has twelve syllables (akshara), so vaishyas become eligible for the sacred-thread at the age of twelve. Shoodras are made of supraphysical energies that are not confined in any meter, and therefore no sacred-thread is required for those in whom this supraphysical energy dominates.

The power of knowledge residing in the mind is Brahma; the power of action residing in prana is kshatriya; the power of 'substance' residing in wak is vaishya; and the power of nourishment residing in poosha is shoodra. Awyaya is the source of all four and, as we noted earlier, mana, prana and wak are three facets or offshoots of awyaya. These are knowledge, action and substance respectively. They become manifest as Brahma, kshatra and vit. The Gita clearly and succinctly states the principle that awyaya is the creator of the four varnas.

As all entities in the universe are produced by the combination of mana, prana and wak, the four varnas are present in all of them, including stones, trees, worms, birds, animals, books, human beings and so forth. Their aggregate creates existence. If we take a book as an example, it is made of a substance, in this case paper. It generates motion when a person reads it, as the ideas in the book 'travel' to its reader. There is an element of durability in the book; it has traits like volume, form and so forth, which are not intrinsic to 'book'. The substance of our book is vaishya, the motion is kshatriya, the durability component is brahmana, and the volume is shoodra.

The Essence of the Ashrama System

The division of the span of a person's life in accordance with specific tasks or goals is the basis of the *ashrama* system. Ishwara comprises the dual power of knowledge and action: Brahma and karma. As all of us emanate from Ishwara, we are also endowed with these two aspects. The aggregation of knowledge and action is manifested in *Om*.

The *ayu* component located in the sun becomes atma, which is permeated with mana, prana and wak. An individual human being is invested with 36,000 units of ayu, and every day we consume one unit of ayu, which includes one unit of mana, one unit of prana and one unit of wak.

Therefore, our lifespan is estimated to be 100 years. The Vedic texts repeatedly state that a person's life extends for 100 years (*shatayur wai purushah*). Of course, it is possible to live longer than that – in very rare cases someone may live up to 400 years. But the ashrama system concerns itself with the normal expected lifespan.

This normal lifespan is divided into two parts, one focusing on the power of knowledge and the other on the power of action. Each of these two portions is further divided into two segments of twenty-five years each. In each part of the total lifespan, the first segment is used for the acquisition of the power of action and the second for the acquisition of the power of knowledge. The segments in an ashrama are called *brahmacharya*, *grihastha*, *vanaprastha* and *sanyasa* respectively.

Knowledge is Brahma. The first segment is devoted to the acquisition of knowledge and is therefore known as *brahmacharya ashrama*. During the first segment, a person belonging to a specific varna acquires knowledge to perform actions which need to be discharged in the second segment. Having completed one's anointed actions, a person enters the third segment in which knowledge, having been validated in the segment of action, is further deepened. This is the segment of *tapa*, of concentrated reflection, endeavour and internalisation. This deepening of knowledge brings the individual to a stage of life where all impulses that led to desires and consequently to actions are 'burnt' in the fire of knowledge.[44]

Actions related to desires are destroyed, but all other actions continue to be performed. 'Although there is no duty for me to fulfil, nor do I have anything to gain, even so I engage myself in the action.'[45] The last segment, devoted wholly to the pursuit of knowledge, is called *sanyasa ashrama*. Having fully lived through the first three segments, the fourth segment becomes a period of inner peace and tranquillity.

NOTES

1. This paragraph was originally published in the second volume of RK Mishra's work, *The Cosmic Matrix: In the Light of the Vedas*, 2001, p.327.
2. This paragraph and the three preceding it were originally published in RK Mishra's first volume, *Before the Beginning and After the End*, 2000, pp.404-405. They are reprinted here in order to provide the reader with a fuller explanation of the important concept of sphota.
3. This paragraph was originally published in the second volume of RK Mishra's work, *The Cosmic Matrix*. Readers are encouraged to read the whole of the chapter 'Veda, Brahmana and *Rishi*', in *The Cosmic Matrix* from which this excerpt was taken, for an exploration of mantra, the principle of Veda and the works themselves which bear the name 'the *Vedas*'.
4. *Laghu Siddhant Kaumudi*, Motilal Banarsidas, Dharanand Shastri, 1991, p.6.
5. This paragraph and the one immediately preceding it were originally published in RK Mishra's third volume, *The Realm of Supraphysics: Mind, Energy and Matter in the Light of the Vedas*, 2003, pp.103-104. Readers are invited to explore the subject of sound, speech and communication from the Vedic viewpoint by reading the whole chapter from which this extract is taken. The chapter is named 'Wak and Communication: Sound, Word, Speech and Language' and is to be found on pages 91 to 115 of *The Realm of Supraphysics*, 2003 edition.
6. *Encyclopedia Britannica*, Internet edition, 2003.
7. *Gita* 8:26.
8. For example, see the translation of verse 4:13 by Boris Marijhovic in his translation of *Geetarth Sangraha* ('Commentary on the *Bhagavadgita*' by Abhinava Gupta).
9. *Brahma Karma,* p.331.
10. *Vrana Varne, Swa. U. Se. / Varna-Prerana P. Se.*, Hindi Geeta Vigyan Bhashya Bhoomika, Vol. II, First Edition, Part B – *Karma Yoga*, p.333.
11. Gita 7:25 – *Karma* 323.
12. Gita 15:16 – *Karma* (334).
13. *Bhagavadgita*, 11 Skanda, Chapter 17 (354 *ibid*).
14. *ibid* 355.
15. *ibid* 355.
16. *Gopatha Brahmana* (*Purana*) 2:23 (356).
17. See *Aitereya Brahmana* 8:1.
18. *Shrimad Bhagwad Purana* 9 Skanda, Chapter 2.
19. *Brahmanyan Chaiv Gadhija, Manusmriti* 7:41, p.357 – *Karmayoga Pareeksha.*
20. *Rig Veda* 10:30:1 (357).
21. *Na Bhaga Risht Puthrou Dwaou Vaishyo Brahamanataam Gatou,*1:11:9, *Harivanshapuranam*, p.34.

22. *Pra Devatra Brahmane Yatu, Rig Veda* 10:30:1 – *Karma Yoga Pareeksha* p.358.
23. *Apanivado javano grahita – Svetasvatara Upanishad,* 1986, with commentary by Shankaracharya, translated by Swami Gambhirananda, p.138.
24. *Sarvatahpanipavan tatsarvato' ksis iromukhan, sarvathasrutimalloke sarvamavrty tishtati – Bhagavadgita,* chapter 13, p.631,in *Sadhaka Sanjivani*, 1995, by Swami Ramsukhdas.
25. *Gayatro Brahmane Nirvart Yat – Geeta Vigyan Bhashya Bhoomika*, Volume II – *Karma Yoga Pareeksha*, p. 359.
26. *Rig Veda* 7:63:4 – *Karma* 40.
27. *Shatpathabrahmana* 14:1:34 – *Karma* 41.
28. *Yajur Veda* 7:42 – *Karma* 42.
29. *Manusmriti* 7:8 – *Karma* 51.
30. *ibid* 7:8 – *Karma* 51.
31. *Karma* 52.
32. *Chaturdwa vihito ha vah agra gni raas – Shatpatha Brahmana,* 1:2:3:1 – *Brahma Karma Pareeksha,* p.322.
33. *Tasya vah atsyagna vargopnisht – Shatpatha Brahmana*, 10:5:1:1 – *Brahma Karma Pareeksha*, p.323.
34. *Poorva Meemamsa* 1:5.
35. *ath vacho vriti vyakhyasyam – Hindi Geeta Vigyan Bhashya Bhoomika*, Vol. II, First Edition, Part B – *Brahma Karma,* p.329.
36. *Brahma Karma* pp.329–330.
37. Monier-Williams, Sir Monier, *Sanskrit-English Dictionary*, 1990, p.583.
38. *ibid* p.580.
39. *Shukla yaju pratishakya*, Chapter 1: 99–101 – *Brahma Karrna* p.333.
40. *Gita* 4:13 – *Brahma Karma* p.333.
41. For a detailed elaboration, please see *The Realm of Supraphysics: Mind, Energy and Matter in the light of the* Vedas by the author.
42. *Tatteriya Upanishad – Karma Yoga* 27.
43. *Shatpatha Brahmana* 14:4:2:23 – *Karma* 29.
44. *Gita* 4:37 – *Karma* 68.
45. *ibid,* 3:22.

SECTION EIGHT

~

EPILOGUE

EPILOGUE

The reflections of Renu Bavejaji in the days and weeks following Mishraji's death seem fitting as a conclusion to this incomplete yet momentous work. We leave our readers to take their own journey onwards in the light of the Vedas.

The fifth and the final book of Mishraji deals with the fragmented mind and its journey towards the Whole Being. We are not what we appear to be, and what we are we do not appear to be. We appear to be the fragmented mind, which is on the surface, but underneath we carry the Universal Being. The whole aim of our life is to discover our true being, our Whole Being. Before departing, through his books, he has made a new beginning in our lives. And he has left his last book open-ended as it was not meant to be summed up. It has not been written because it could not be written. This was a decision not just of Mishraji but a decision of his Whole Being.

While going through the chapter 'Consciousness: Individual and Universal' once again, it is confirmed to me that this book is COMPLETE. Every syllable, every word, every sentence and every chapter is complete in itself. Each and every part is beaming with 'wholeness'.

A diamond when seen from any side will appear as a diamond, providing there is nothing obstructing our vision. It may appear to be a stone if there is a little clouding; and when our view is completely blocked we will not be able to see it, even though it is fully present and sparkling.

Just one word explains the entire book – wholeness. Be with this word, concentrate on it, contemplate, meditate, do whatever that takes you to the inner depths of this word. Reading this book will enable you to touch the wholeness of every atom on the earth – sentient or insentient. We are whole; each and every cell of our body is a whole. This book not only enables realisation of the wholeness of our being; it is also a tool to help us to manifest the wholeness that is embedded in every part of our being. This is the only karma, this is the only dharma and the only purpose of life on earth. Everything on the earth is not *a part* of the whole – it *is* whole. The very presence of every cell and atom here is to manifest its true nature. This wholeness is waiting for us to become conscious of its inherent reality so that it can emerge in its true form – not merely as realisation but as physical manifestation as well.

The true seekers of life will attempt this question and answer it with their lives. The remaining part of *The Whole Being*, therefore, has been left to each one of us to write on ourselves, to action in our lives, to be that and to discover our Whole Being. This task has to be taken up seriously, in fact with the same seriousness with which Mishraji wrote all his books, in the later period of his life.

Knowledge, he has given to us in abundance. His

'unfinished' book carries a hidden meaning for us to decipher in our own individual way. To me, it means that the time has come on the earth to translate all the knowledge we have gained into action; to discover our Whole Being and allow it to live its natural life. This is the sole purpose of our existence and this is our very destiny.

To experience the power and boundlessness of our dear Mishraji, we have to be ready to transcend the boundaries of our fragmented minds and embark upon the journey of the 'unknown', with his known hand to assist us. Here alone we shal! find the fulfillment of our being and the being of the great soul. He is here and shall continue to live until eternity, not just for the sake of knowledge but for the sake of 'knowledge in action'.

As far as the book is concerned, it is complete. But when it comes to us, we can see that a mammoth unfinished task is lying ahead of us. The guidance is there. Knowing our wholeness and the potential we carry, it is now up to each one of us to take it upon ourselves to materialise the divine consciousness lying dormant and latent in the depths of each and every cell of our being.

Before leaving, he announced his departure. It was a conscious decision. Then how could he leave his work undone?

✦

I came in contact with Mishraji sometime in 1987 and worked closely with him for a year and a half when he was chairman of the Observer Group of Publications. During this period I came to discover the other side of his life – his true being. I left the Observer *in 1992, a year that marked the beginning of a new chapter in my life in which I was initiated by Mishraji. One year of extensive studies and his personal guidance opened new horizons. He introduced me to myself, and enabled me to stand on my own two feet so that I could walk on my own into the new world. After this, many years went by during which I met him only twice. Probably it was not required any more as the seed was sown, so his absence was never felt. Even today, when he has left his body, I see no change. For me, he is still here. In fact, he is more real than earlier. He has gone beyond the limits of his mind and body and has emerged even stronger in his real form.*

Renu Baveja

Appendix 1

THE FABRIC OF WHOLENESS

(FROM ELEMENTS TO UNIVERSAL CONSCIOUSNESS)

THE 36 TATTWAS OF THE UNIVERSE

According to Kashmiri Shaivism, our universe exists and functions by 36 tattwas. The term 'tattwa' signifies essence, or the fundamental factor from which something evolves. This Appendix lists these 36 tattwas, which are inextricably intertwined and interdependent but which, for the purposes of explanation only, we can divide into the following categories:

Five Gross Material Elements

Earth (*Prithvi*)
Water (*Jala*)
Fire (*Tejas*)
Air (*Vayu*)
Ether (*Akasha*)

Five Subtle Elements

Smell (*Gandha*)
Taste (*Rasa*)

Form (*Rupa*)
Touch (*Sparsa*)
Sound (*Shabda*)

Five Organs of Action
Speech (*Wak*)
Hand (*Pani*)
Foot (*Pada*)
Excretion (*Payu*)
Creativity (*Upastha*)

Five Organs of Cognition
Nose, organ of smelling (*Ghrana*)
Tongue, organ of tasting (*Rasana*)
Eye, organ of seeing (*Chaksu*)
Skin, organ of touching (*Twak*)
Ear, organ of hearing (*Srotra*)

Three Internal Organs
Mind (*Manas*)
Intellect (*Buddhi*)
Ego connected with objectivity (*Ahamkara*)

Nature/ego
Nature (*Prakriti*)
Ego connected with subjectivity (*Purusha*)

Six Coverings or Limitations
Limitation of creativity (*Kala*)
Limitation of knowledge (*Vidya*)
Limitation of attachment (*Raga*)

Limitation of time (*Kaala*)
Limitation of place (*Niyati*)
Illusion of individuality (*Maya*)

Pure Elements

Pure subjectivity (*Suddha Vidya*)
Pure subjectivity (*Ishvara*)
Subjectivity in its pure form (*Sadasiva*, *Shakti*)
Being (*Parama Shiva*)

'The last is that Being which does not come in the cycle of tattwas. That Being is called Parama Shiva. Parama Shiva is not only found in Shiva tattwa, nor only found in Shakti tattwa. It is not only here. It is not only there. Everywhere you will find it. You will find it in the lowest tattwa to the highest tattwa. It is at all levels. That is why it is at no level. It is everywhere. That is why it is nowhere.'[1]

---

1 Lakshmanjoo, Swami. *Kashmiri Shaivism: The Secret Supreme*, Srinagar: Universal Shaiva Trust, p.10, 1985.

Appendix 2

A BRIEF BIOGRAPHY OF ABHINAVAGUPTA

The author wishes to acknowledge that the following information about the great sage and proponent of Kashmiri Shaivism, Abhinavagupta, is summarised from Mark Dyczkowski's seminal work on Kashmiri Shaivism, *The Doctrine of Vibration*.

Abhinavagupta lived in Kashmir from about the middle of the tenth century into the eleventh. His ancestors were distinguished scholars in the court of Kanauj, and were brought to Kashmir by King Lalitaditya around the middle of the eighth century.

He was, without a doubt, the most brilliant of all teachers of Kashmiri Shaivism. He was also one of the greatest spiritual and intellectual giants to whom India has given birth. In his life he wrote more than 60 works, some of which were extensive, and all of which were remarkable for the beauty of their Sanskrit expression and the profundity of their thought.

Perhaps Abhinavagupta's most important work is *Tantraloka* ('The Light of the Tantras'), while his commentary on Anandavardhana's *Dhvanyaloka* ('Mirror of Suggestion') is also famous; in this work, Anandavardhana and Abhinavagupta expound the theory that the soul of poetry is its power of suggestion, through which sentiment is conveyed to the reader. His commentary on the *Natyashastra*, the foremost treatise in Sanskrit dramaturgy, is the only one to be preserved, a fact that testifies to its excellence and influence. In the later period of his life, Abhinavagupta wrote extensive and profound commentaries on Utpaladeva's stanzas in *Isvarapratyabhijnakarika* (Recognition of God). In these commentaries, he elucidates the Doctrine of Recognition (*pratyabhijna*).

Abhinavagupta interprets the dialogue between Shiva and Parvati as a dialogue within our own consciousness, that is, between the two levels of consciousness, whereby it appears to divide itself into the one asking the questions and the one answering them, both being itself at the same time. In other words, the dialogue is between the seeking self and the answering self, the answer being provided from within the Self. The questioning self is the lower self (*anu*) and the answering self is the higher Self (*Shiva*). The same interpretation may be given to the dialogue between Arjuna and Krishna in Bhagavadgita.

The works of Abhinavagupta can be divided into his commentaries and his independent works. His commentaries are as follows:

1. *Isvara-pratyabhijna-vimarsini* (*laghvi vrtti*). A commentary on the *Isvara-pratyabhijna-karika* of Utpaladeva.
2. *Isvara-pratyabhijna-vivrti-vimarsini* (*brhati vrtti*). A larger commentary on the *Isvara-pratyabhijna-karika*

of Utpaladeva, based on the lost commentary of Utpala.

3. *Paratrimsika-vivarana*. A commentary on *Paratrimsika*.
4. *Bhagavadgitartha-sangraha*. A short commentary on the *Gita*.
5. *Sivadrstyalocana*. A commentary on the *Siva-drsti* of Somananda (not available).

His independent works are:

1. *Tantraloka*, his magnum opus. This huge work presents the philosophy, religion and yogic sadhana of the non-dual Shiva-Tantric tradition, Kashmiri Shaivism. The *Tantraloka* was first published along with the *Viveka* by the Kashmir Series of Texts and Studies, Srinagar, in twelve volumes. It is composed in verse.
2. *Tantrasara*. A prose summary of the main topics of the *Tantraloka*.
3. *Tantra-vata-dhanika*. A further summarisation, in verse, of the *Tantraloka*, which is like the seed (*dhanika*) of the banyan tree (*vata*) of tantra.
4. *Malinivijaya-vartika*. An extensive exposition of the *Malinivijayottara Tantra*.
5. *Paramarthasara*. A non-dualistic rendering of Sesa Muni's semi-dualistic work, the *Adhara-karikas*.

Apart form the above-mentioned works, Abhinavagupta wrote a number of short works, including his *stotra*s. Some of these, such as the *Anuttarastika*, contain profound philosophical wisdom. They are as follows:

1. *Anuttarastika*
2. *Paramartha-dvadasika*
3. *Paramartha-charca*
4. *Mahopadesa-vimsatikam*
5. *Kramastotram*
6. *Bhairava-stavah* (*Bhairava-stotram*)
7. *Dehastha-devata-cakra-stotram*
8. *Anubhava-nivedanam*

In addition to these works of philosophy, religion and yogic practice, Abhinavagupta composed two influential works on poetics in commentary form. Although the topic of these two works is aesthetics, they both have a philosophical background. In both works, but most notably in his commentary on the *Natyashastra*, Abhinavagupta presents the Indian aesthetic theory from the point of view of the spiritual philosophy of Shaivism. These two works are:

1. *Dhvanyaloka-locana*. A commentary on the *Dhvanyaloka* of Anandavardhana, a work expounding on the *vyanjana* or suggestion theory of Indian poetics.
2. *Abhinava-bharati*. A commentary on the famous *Natyashastra* of Bharata, expounding on the Indian theory of *rasa* or aesthetic enjoyment.

GLOSSARY

agni	fire; a primary supraphysical energy.
agnihotra	a ceremony consisting of offering oblations to fire.
ahamkara [aha⁄k⁄ra]	the concept of 'I'; the individualised ego-consciousness.
akasha [⁄k⁄sa]	the first of the five gross material elements; space generated by antariksha (the separation of heaven and earth), the principal space being a continuous, unbounded extension in every direction.
akshara [ak⁄ara]	imperishable; unalterable.
ambhrini [ambh⁄⁄i]	wak related to parmeshthi; also known as 'ambhrini wak'.
amrita [am⁄ta]	Immortal; unperishable; the unchanging principle in an individual, as distinguished from the ever-changing principles.
ananda	that which consumes anna (fire in relation to fuel); unalloyed joy; pure bliss.
antaryami [antary⁄m⁄]	that which determines the innate nature of every individual; the regulatory factor at the heart of the universe.
arhat	one who has attained individual liberation or enlightenment.

artha	substance; wealth; content captured in a word (shabda).
ashrama [⁄srama]	a 25-year 'segment' of a 100-year human lifespan.
asura	generally translated as demons or opponents of the gods; a class of supraphysical energy.
atma [⁄tm⁄]	indivisible; unlimited; the all-pervasive and indestructible substratum of every individual, erroneously translated as 'spirit'; ultimate identity; also known as 'atman'.
atman	see 'atma'.
awyakta	unmanifest; an entity or being in its pre-manifest stage.
awyaya	the unlimited source of all supraphysical energies; the ultimate cause of creation of the material universe.
bala	the first formation in the process of creation when rasa, the vast limitless stillness, is stirred and a unifying principle begins to divide itself into separate and diverse units of supraphysical energy.
bhairava	the divine form of the Absolute.
Bharatavarsha [bh⁄ratvar⁄a]	the region between the Himalayas and the Indian Ocean.
bodhisattva	an enlightened being who, out of compassion, forgoes personal nirvana in order to bring others to liberation.
Brahma [brahm⁄]	the foundation or basis of the totality

	of the created universe; this universe is another manifestation of Brahma.
Brahman [brahma⁄]	the ultimate source from which this entire creation of sentient and insentient beings originates, exists and finally merges into; a portion of the text of the vedas which elucidate the application of vigyan (scientific principles).
brahmana [br⁄ma⁄a]	priest; one of the four sections in which society was organised in Bharatavarsha.
buddhi	intellect; the faculty of awake-ness or awareness; the power of forming and retaining concepts and general notions; intelligence.
chandrama [chandram⁄]	moon; one of the five individuals in the cosmic pattern (the other four are prithwi, soorya, parmeshthi and swayambhoo).
chhanda	meter; one of the six branches of the Vedas.
chit	the thinking principle; the seat of intellective functions; mind viewed as seat or organ; the aggregate of cognitive, volitional and emotional activities and processes of the individual; also spelt 'chitta'.
darshana [dar⁄ana]	seeing; looking; observing; perception; doctrines or philosophical systems.
devata [devat⁄]	a specific class of supraphysical energies, as distinct from asura, which emerges from the same source.

dharma	merit. This is the comprehensive term that reflects the blending of ethics, duty, characteristics and properties of an individual.
dharmin	substance.
dhwani	seamless sound; echo; tune; also spelt 'dhvani'.
dwija	'twice-born', one who has gone through the thread ceremony.
gandharva	a class of entities; a species different from human beings, generally regarded as celestial musicians or heavenly singers.
gayatri [g/yatr/] (meter)	the incoming supraphysical energy of prana returning and passing through the earth; a type of meter (chhanda) of 24 syllables, variously arranged but purely as a triplet of eight syllables each; the name of the popular and powerful mantra. Literally translated, it means 'that which protects whoever chants it.'
guna [gu/a]	constituent process; trait; attribute.
Ishwara [i/wara]	the supreme principle which regulates the universe, comprising all disparate individuals (jeeva regulates individuals and Ishwara regulates jeevas).
jagati [jagat/]	a type of meter (chhanda) of 4 x 12 syllables.
jati [j/ti]	species; universal attribute; erroneously translated as 'caste' or 'race'.
jeeva [jiva]	the supreme principle which regulates

	an individual, often applied to a living being; individualised consciousness.
jnana [j⁄ ⁄na]	consciousness; knowledge; awareness.
karma	action; work; pure movement in consciousness.
Krishna [k⁄ ⁄ ⁄a]	a cosmic phenomenon; in the Puranas, Krishna is the eighth avatar of Vishnu; black, or dark as a cloud.
kshara [ksara]	the immediate supraphysical source from which the material universe and cosmic individuals evolve; literally, 'destructible'.
kshatriya [k⁄atriya]	one of the four sections in which Asian society was organised historically.
lakshmi [lak⁄m⁄]	symbol of prosperity; the glow of the illuminating power of the sun; the 'wife' of Vishnu.
madhyama [madhyam⁄]	between the two levels of speech (vaikharee and pashyanti) there is a middle level known as 'madhyama vac' – the level of thought. Its association is chiefly with buddhi.
mana	one of the three components of atma, the other two being prana and wak; also translated as 'mind' or 'heart'.
mantra	a verse in the Vedas; the words in which the seer-scientists articulated their discoveries of the processes of nature, the cosmos and beyond.
matrikachakram [matrik⁄chakram]	'wheel of the alphabet'.

matrika-shakti [matrika⁄akti]	the power of the letters of the alphabet.
maya [m⁄y⁄]	an extraordinary power, which emanates from the infinite and makes possible the interplay of finite phenomena.
mudra [mudr⁄]	seal; stamp; a series of symbolic body postures and hand movements used in East Indian classical dancing; arm, hand and body positions used in the traditions of Hinduism and Buddhism.
pada	a method of chanting the Veda mantras; one-quarter of a mantra or a stanza.
panchamahabhootas [panchamah⁄bh⁄ta]	the five gross material elements of earth (prithvi), water (jala), fire (teja), wind/air (vayu) and space (akasha).
parabrahma	the eternal principle in which the attributes of all individuals of the cosmos are subsumed.
para pashyanti-rupa	the pure, basic language principle.
parmeshthi [parme⁄thi]	the prajapati which orbits around Brahma and is filled with apa; also one dimension of the five-dimensional universe, the other four being swayambhoo, soorya, chandrama and prithvi.
parmeshwara [parme⁄wara]	the supreme principle in which all Ishwaras are subsumed.
pashu [also pasu]	a supraphysical energy which creates all material substance.
pashyanti [pa⁄yant⁄]	the inner idea, or sphota (see separate entry), is aptly designated as

	'pashyanti vac' – the intuitive flash of understanding of a sentence, book or poem as a whole. Pashyanti is the direct experience of the vakya sphota, of meaning as in the numeral whole.
pati	the master of creation.
pitara	translated as 'ancestors' or 'forefathers'; technically, one of the several unchangeable supraphysical energies; also written as 'pitra'.
prakasha [prak//a]	the substratum of manifestation; light; illumination; the pure light of consciousness.
prakriti [prak/ti]	nature; literally, 'the state prior to the manifestation of objects'; primordial materiality.
prama	cognitive awareness; true.
prana [pr//a]	vital energy; supraphysical energy; life-force; breath.
pratibha [pratibh/]	to shine upon; to come inside; a flash (upon thoughts); splendour; an image; intelligence; spontaneous manifestation; awareness; intuition.
prithwi [p/thwi]	the earth, one of the five gross material elements; also spelt 'prithvi'.
purusha [puru/a]	the immutable source from which mutable nature emanates; the ultimate manifested 'ocean' of energy, which is observable as differentiated, variegated nature.
rasa	juice; fluid; vast, limitless stillness; the

best, finest or prime part of anything; essence; marrow; taste.

rishi [⁄⁄i] — a supraphysical energy which comes into motion spontaneously; a seer-scientist who discovers a specific supraphysical energy.

ritwik [⁄twik] — a person who has a profound knowledge of *Rig Veda*.

sama — the extent to which an individual or an entity can be seen; one of the four Vedas (*Sama Veda*).

samadhi [sam⁄dhi] — intense and prolonged concentration of the mind leading to total absorption in the Self.

samvid — pure consciousness alone; instantaneous communication.

sanatana dharma [san⁄tana dharma] — a way of life based on certain eternal (sanatana) principles, which include ethics, duties, responsibilities, relationships, and a comprehensive world view.

Saraswati [saraswat⁄] — the goddess of learning, a vast network of rivers with that name.

sat — truth; enduring; unchangeable; stable.

savita [savit⁄] — the direct luminosity of the sun; the luminous rays radiating from the mass of every individual.

savitri [s⁄vitr⁄] — the supraphysical energy radiating from savita.

shabda [⁄abda] — sound; word.

shakti [⁄akti] — the supraphysical power and energy

	which govern the world; the power of Shiva; in grammar, the significative power of words.
sheela [shila]	morality.
Shiva [/iva]	the supraphysical energy of peace and well-being; the ultimate all-pervasive reality principle which manifests in the form of the five energies of consciousness, will, knowledge, action and bliss; fundamental reality or the Absolute.
shoodra [//dra]	one of the four sections in which Asian society was organised historically.
shukla [/ukla]	white.
shunya [/unya]	nothingness; the symbol zero; void; empty.
shunyata [/unyat/]	commonly translated as 'emptiness', shunyata is the essence of reality and of experience; egolessness.
soma	the material cause of the universe; a specific category of supraphysical energy.
soorya [s/rya]	the sun.
spanda	the inner universal vibration of consciousness; divine power.
sphota [spho/a]	the sentence taken as an integral symbol.
sutra [s/tra]	thread; an aphorism containing essential truths expounded by the seer-scientists or by the Buddha.
swara	vowel; sound; note.
tamas	the trait of inertia, one of the three gunas.

tanmatra [tanm/tr/]	an element (water, earth, air, fire and space) in its pure natural state, before it manifests on a gross level.
tattwa	essence; the fundamental factor from which something evolves; also written as 'tatwa'.
teja	the sun; light; fire; extremely subtle, upward-moving, expansive prana.
trishtup [tri//up]	a type of meter (chhanda), every line of which carries eleven letters.
tureeya [turiya]	a fourth plane of consciousness, wherein reality is one and indivisible; an expansive state of consciousness during the differentiated states of waking, dreaming and deep sleep.
vaikharee [vaikhari]	the outer speaking of words and sentences; the uttered sounds which combine to make up the sentence, book or poem.
vaishya [vai/ya]	one of the four sections in which Asian society was organised historically.
vakya [v/kya]	sentence; synthetic connection.
varna [var/a]	the principle and application of varna; letters of the alphabets, phenomena; four sections in which society was organised in ancient India.
veerya [virya]	creative vitality.
vid	to know; knowledge; to discover; to acquire; to experience.
visarga	the universal state wherein the three energies of will, knowledge and action

	are fused into one universal point.
Vishnu [vi⁄⁄u]	a supraphysical energy.
vyanjana [vyanjan⁄]	consonants; one of several ways to find out what a word seeks to convey; allusion; figurative expression; indicative meaning.
wak [w⁄k]	language; speech; the substance in an object; the matter within the shell.
yajaman [yajam⁄na]	a person who organises a yajnya.
yajnya [yajny⁄]	the interaction and fusion of supraphysical energies and/or material substances; the process of the acculturation of agni; the refinement and embellishment of agni.

BIBLIOGRAPHY

Bohm, David. *The Undivided Universe: An Ontological Interpretation of Quantum Theory* (posthumous work), London: Routledge, 1993.

Bohm, David. *Wholeness and the Implicate Order*, London: Routledge, 1980.

Bortoft, Henri. *The Wholeness of Nature: Goethe's Way of Science*, Edinburgh: Floris Books, 1996.

Causton, Richard. *The Buddha in Daily Life: An Introduction to the Buddhism of Nichiren Daishonin*, UK: Rider & Co, 1995.

Coats, Callum. *Living Energies, An Exposition of Concepts Related to the Theories of Viktor Schauberger*, Dublin: Gateway Publications (Gill & Macmillan Ltd), 2001.

Dyczkowski, Mark S G. *The Doctrine of Vibration*, USA: State University of New York Press, 1987.

Elias, Norbert. *The Society of Individuals* (poem translated by Michael Hamburger), Cambridge: Continuum International Publishing Group, 2001.

Fundamentals of Buddhism. Tokyo: Yasuji Krimura, Nichiren Shoshu International Center, 1977.

Gambhirananda, Swami (tr.). *Svetasvatara Upanishad: with commentary by Shankaracharya*, Mayavati, Pitoragarh: Swami, Ananyanand, President Advaita Ashram, 1986.

Hindi Geeta Vigyan Bhashya Bhoomika, Vol. II, first edition, Part B, Kolkata: Seth Surajmal Jalan Smrit Mandir Library.

Hughes, John. *Self Realization in Kashmir Shaivism:* The Oral Teachings of Swami Lakshman Joo, Delhi: Sri Satguru Publications, 1997.

Lakshmanjoo, Swami. *Shiva Sutras: The Supreme Awakening.* California: Universal Shaiva Fellowship, 2002.

Lisagor, Michael. *Romancing the Buddha*, Santa Monica, USA: Middleway Press, 2005.

Mishra, Rishi Kumar. *The Ultimate Dialogue: the Fusion of Knowledge, Intelligence and Action,* Delhi: Rupa & Co in association with Brahma Vidya Kendra, 2007.

Mishra, Rishi Kumar. *The Realm of Supraphysics: Mind, Energy and Matter in the Light of the Vedas*, Delhi: Rupa & Co in association with Brahma Vidya Kendra, 2003.

Mishra, Rishi Kumar. *The Cosmic Matrix*, Delhi: Rupa & Co in association with Brahma Vidya Kendra, 2001.

Mishra, Rishi Kumar. *Before the Beginning and After the End*, Delhi: Rupa & Co. in association with Brahma Vidya Kendra, 2000.

Monier-Williams, Sir Monier. *A Sanskrit-English Dictionary*, Delhi: Motilal Banarsidas Publishers Ltd, 1990.

Naydler, Jeremy (ed.). *Goethe On Science: An Anthology of Goethe's Scientific Writings*, Edinburgh: Floris Books, 1996.

Peat, F David. *Infinite Potential: The Life and Times of David Bohm*, Reading, MA: Addison Wesley, 1997.

Ramsukhdas, Swami. *Sadhaka Sanjivani* (a commentary on *Bhagavadgita*), third edition, Govind Bhavan Karyalay, Gorakhpur: Geeta Press, 1995.

Roshi, Shunryu Suzuki. *Zen Mind, Beginners Mind*, New York & Tokyo: John Weatherhill, (first ed. 1970), 1980.

Schad, Wolfgang. *Man and Mammals: Toward a Biology of Form*, New York: Waldorf Press, 1977.

Shri *Harivanshapuranam* Part I, Kolkata: Nag Publishers.

Soka Gakkai. *The Soka Gakkai Dictionary of Buddhism*, Japan: 2002.

Soka Gakkai. *The Writings of Nichiren Daishonin*, Vol.1, Japan: 1999.

Vrana Varne, Swa. U. Se./Varna-Prerana P. Se., Hindi Geeta Vigyan Bhashya Bhoomika, Vol. II, first edition, Part B, Kolkata: Seth Surajmal Jalan Smrit Mandir Library.

INDEX